TABLE OF CONTENTS

The LORD gave and the Lord has taken away;
may the name of the LORD be praised (1:21).

— 1 —
A Man Whose
Name Was Job
Job 1–2

DIMENSION ONE:
WHAT DOES THE BIBLE SAY?

Answer these questions by reading Job 1

1. What kind of person is Job? (1:1)

2. Why is Job called "the greatest man among all the people of the East"? (1:2-3)

3. How do Job's children spend their time? (1:4)

4. What does Job do continually on behalf of his children? Why? (1:5)

5. Of what group is Satan a part? (1:6)

6. How does Satan occupy his time? (1:7)

7. What does the Lord ask Satan? (1:8)

8. What does Satan say God has done for Job? (1:9-10)

9. What is Satan's challenge to God? (1:11)

10. Does God accept Satan's challenge? If so, what limitations does God place on Satan? (1:12)

11. What calamities befall Job?

_____ (1:14-15)

_____ (1:16)

_____ (1:17)

_____ (1:18-19)

12. What does Job do in response to these tragic events? (1:20)

13. What does Job say? (1:21-22)

Answer these questions by reading Job 2

14. Why does God consider Job vindicated? (2:3)

15. What does Satan tell God to do? (2:4-5)

16. What condition does God attach to Satan's second challenge? (2:6)

17. How does Satan afflict Job? (2:7)

18. What advice does Job's wife offer? (2:9)

19. What is Job's response to this advice? (2:10)

20. Who are the friends who come to console Job? (2:11)

21. What do Job's friends do when they first see Job? (2:12-13)

22. What do Job's friends say to him? Why? (2:13)

DIMENSION TWO:
WHAT DOES THE BIBLE MEAN?

❑ *Job 1:1.* Various meanings have been suggested for the Hebrew name *Job*, including hostile, persecuted, enemy, or hated one. In fact, *Job* may have been a common proper name with no special symbolic significance. Uz, the country of Job's origin, is probably Edom. As an Edomite, Job would have been a descendant of Esau, Jacob's brother, and therefore a non-Israelite or Gentile.

Job is described as "blameless [from a Hebrew word meaning complete or whole] and upright" (that is, absolutely honest and fair in his dealings with others). The term *feared God* refers not only to a sense of God's awesomeness but also to a strict and scrupulous obedience to God's law. (See Deuteronomy 6:1-3.)

❑ *Job 1:2.* Job's wealth and large family are evidence that Job is highly favored by God. Sons in particular were considered a reward for righteousness. (See Psalm 127:3-5.)

❑ *Job 1:4-5.* The reference to how Job's sons "used to take turns holding feasts" may mean that they feasted daily—each of the seven sons having one day of the week! In any case, the feasting was frequent. So Job was constantly taking precautions to ensure his children's righteous status before God. To "curse God in [one's] heart" means to think of God in a disrespectful or contemptuous manner.

❑ *Job 1:6.* "Angels" translates the Hebrew term for "sons of God" and refers here to members of an angelic court who regularly present themselves before God. They are servants ready to do God's bidding. One of this company is Satan (literally, *the* Satan). Taken from a verb meaning to accuse, the term *Satan* is used here as a title and not as a proper name. The function performed by this accuser, or adversary, is similar to that of a criminal investigator or prosecuting attorney.

❑ *Job 1:7-8.* The verb translated here as "going back and forth" should be understood in the sense of patroling or being on the lookout for someone to accuse. The reference to Job as God's servant places him in the company of Israel's greatest heroes: Moses, Caleb, David, Isaiah, Zerubbabel, and others.

❑ *Job 1:9-12.* "Does Job fear God for nothing?" (The *Contemporary English Version* asks, "Why shouldn't he respect you?"[1]) The Accuser challenges God by suggesting that Job's righteousness is really in his own self-interest. God has rewarded Job's obedience with great wealth and has "put a hedge around" (that is, protected) him, his family, and his possessions. God should test Job's faithfulness by withdrawing that hedge and allowing Job to suffer. The Accuser predicts that, under duress, Job will curse God (commit blasphemy). God cannot ignore this affront to Job's honor and God's credibility. The Accuser may test Job so long as Job himself is not harmed.

❑ *Job 1:13-19.* In a single day, a series of catastrophes deprives Job of his livestock, his servants, and his children. The Sabeans are Arabian nomads who send marauding bands northward into Uz. The "fire of God" is lightning. Chaldeans are nomads of Aramean origin who approach Uz from the east and north. Finally, Job's children are killed in a whirlwind. Job is left with absolutely nothing, except his health.

❑ *Job 1:20-22.* The tearing of garments and shaving of one's head are customary signs of mourning in Oriental societies. Despite this total devastation, Job continues to worship God in the traditional fashion by prostrating himself full-length on the ground. Contrary to the Accuser's expectation, Job's prayer shows him faithfully to accept his misfortune. Instead of cursing God, Job blesses God!

❑ *Job 2:1-3.* The heavenly court reconvenes, and God again boasts to the Accuser about Job. Unjustly accused and victimized, Job "maintains his integrity."

❑ *Job 2:4.* "Skin for skin" is a proverbial saying of uncertain meaning. ("Value for value" or "a life for a life" have been suggested paraphrases.) The sentence immediately following—"A man will give all he has for his own life."—is our best clue. The Accuser thinks the stakes are not yet high enough. Were Job's own body to be touched, he would indeed curse God. Once again God agrees to the test, giving the Accuser permission to afflict Job in the flesh but not to kill him.

❑ *Job 2:7-8.* Job is now tormented with a hideous disease of the skin that covers his entire body with malignant ulcers and boils. This condition requires Job to isolate himself, so he retires to the equivalent of the town dump—a heap of dust, ashes, and dirt found at the entrance of ancient Near Eastern villages.

❏ *Job 2:9-10.* Job's wife, who appears only once in the story, gives way to despair and advises Job to curse God and die. She is telling Job, Your situation is hopeless; put yourself out of your misery! Angry at her effort to sway him, Job accuses his wife of moral weakness. The *Contemporary English Version* translates his response, "If we accept blessings from God, we must accept trouble as well."[2] Just as before, Job's suffering does not shake his faith. He utters no curse against God.

❏ *Job 2:11-13.* Job's three friends hear of his misfortune and arrive together to comfort him. However, Job has been so disfigured by grief and disease that he is no longer recognizable. Shocked and horrified, they also perform ritual acts of mourning. Without uttering a word, they sit by Job for seven days and nights, waiting for him to speak.

DIMENSION THREE:
WHAT DOES THE BIBLE MEAN TO ME?

The Prologue to Job (Chapters 1– 2) introduces us immediately to the book's major issues: strict retribution and innocent suffering. Discussion of these issues begins with the first lesson and will continue throughout the study. An appropriate way to prepare for these discussions is to reflect on your own previous encounters with the Book of Job. Ask yourself, *What will reading the Book of Job mean to me?*

Everyone wants to read Job—or at least everyone feels he or she should want to read Job—because great claims are made for this book. We know that Job is a book about heroic patience and faith in the face of intense and undeserved suffering. Many of us approach Job with the cautious hope that we are finally going to learn something conclusive about the meaning and mystery of evil, injustice, and innocent suffering.

If you are like most persons, your expectations about Job have been shaped more by hearsay than by actual experience with the book. What have you heard about Job? What do you know? When have you last read (or tried to read) Job? How old were you? How much personal suffering had you experienced or witnessed by that time? What do you remember about the experience of reading Job? What particular problems of content did you encounter? Were you part of a group, or were you working on your own?

For most of us, our primary contact with Scripture occurs on Sunday morning. What have you learned about Job as a result of participation in public worship? When did you last hear Scripture read from Job or a sermon preached on Job? How has preaching shaped your vision of Job? Is this vision appealing?

Make a list of the suggestions your image of Job (the man and the book) suggests. Keep this list for future reference.

Job 1:9—Strict Retribution

When the Accuser asks the question, "Does Job fear God for nothing?" he is assuming a view of divine justice that is often referred to as the doctrine of strict retribution. We see this perspective reflected in much biblical literature (but especially in Deuteronomy and Proverbs). This view assumes that the person who (like Job) is scrupulously observant of God's law will also (like Job) be blessed with long life, offspring, and wealth. And, the person who conducts his or her life without regard for God—the person who sins out of either ignorance or malice—will suffer from poverty, ill health, and social isolation. Put bluntly, this doctrine states that, sooner or later, we get what we deserve!

The contemporary Christian probably finds this statement a little crass and more than a little simplistic. Simple observation tells us that many good and pious people die young, remain poor, and fail to achieve any significant social status. Moreover, we are also aware of people who prosper despite their unethical lifestyles. Our first reaction to the doctrine of strict retribution is confidently to assert that it does not work.

A more important question for us to consider is whether we want it to work! Would this be a better world if all God-fearing folk were amply and visibly rewarded for living faithfully? Would this be a better world if all sinners got what they deserve?

Job is presented in the Prologue (Chapters 1–2) as the ideal of ancient piety. Is Job an equally good model for Christian piety today? Is there such a thing as a "model" Christian? If so, how would you describe such a person? What marks of God's blessing (if any) would you expect to see exhibited in the model Christian's life?

Do Christians expect to get what they deserve? Do Christians expect God to behave in a predictable fashion? If so, how? How can we love, trust, and obey a God who is free to give us absolutely nothing in return?

Job 2:6—Innocent Suffering

What do you think of the God who permits Job to suffer? Do you find this God cruel, capricious, unjust, or simply inscrutable? Do you find yourself saying, "This is not the God I believe in."?

Stop a minute and reflect on the biblical witness as a whole. Does the Bible generally exclude the possibility of innocent suffering? Read Genesis 22 and Luke 4:1-13. These are accounts of two of the most faithful and obedient people ever to draw breath. Yet God permits them to be tempted in a way that causes great suffering. (In Luke, as in Job, the agent of temptation is something other than God.)

The Bible contains numerous stories about or allusions to a God who permits innocent suffering, most often as a consequence of some form of testing. In the two accounts mentioned above, there is not concern to explain or justify the need for these tests. God's freedom to test is absolute. The author of Job is really much more sympathetic to the reader's needs. We are provided at the outset with an explanation for God's actions. In the context of this particular story, God has a good reason for permitting suffering to occur. You, the reader, are told this reason. But Job, the innocent sufferer, is never told!

What are God's options? God can refuse to allow the testing to occur and thus "live with" the possibility that Job does indeed serve God out of self-interest. The Accuser's challenge may be allowed to stand, sullying the reputation of Job and

God alike. But doesn't God know that Job is faithful in the purest sense of the word? Not if Job is a free agent. The freedom bestowed on humanity in Creation allows us to serve God freely as a matter of choice.

God's other option is to trust Job to respect that freedom and to allow the context of the relationship to be drastically altered. Under the circumstances, what does Job deserve? Does he deserve to be spared or to be vindicated?

How much freedom do we exercise in our service to God? To what extent would we be willing to protect this freedom? Can God presume our faith? Looking back over experiences that have tested or tried you, do you feel resentful for having been tested? If so, what caused these feelings of resentment?

---

[1] From the *Contemporary English Version*; Copyright © American Bible Society 1991.
[2] From the *Contemporary English Version*; Copyright © American Bible Society 1991.

Should not your piety
be your confidence? (4:6).

2

The Terrors of God
Job 3–7

DIMENSION ONE:
WHAT DOES THE BIBLE SAY?

Answer these questions by reading Job 3

1. What does Job wish? (3:1-10)

2. Why does Job wish he had died in infancy? (3:11-19)

3. What is Job's accusation against God? (3:20-26)

Answer these questions by reading Job 4

4. How did Job always treat the weak and unfortunate? (4:1-6)

5. Now that Job is the sufferer, what should be the basis of his hope? (4:6)

6. What is the fate of those who "plow evil"? (4:7-11)

7. What message did Eliphaz receive in a night vision? (4:12-21)

Answer these questions by reading Job 5

8. What does Eliphaz claim is the source of human trouble and affliction? (5:1-7)

9. What is Eliphaz's personal advice to Job? Why? (5:8-16)

10. What does Eliphaz say will be the end result of God's chastening of Job? (5:17-27)

Answer these questions by reading Job 6

11. Whom does Job blame for his troubles? (6:1-4)

12. What does Job beg God to do? (6:8-13)

13. What changes does Job see in his friends? (6:14-23)

14. What does Job ask his friends? (6:24-30)

Answer these questions by reading Job 7

15. To what does Job compare human life? (7:1-6)

16. What does Job believe will be his ultimate fate? (7:7-10)

17. Job asks God many questions. What is the one thing he asks over and over? (7:11-21)

DIMENSION TWO:
WHAT DOES THE BIBLE MEAN?

❑ *Job 3:1-10.* After seven days and nights of silence, Job finally opens his mouth with a jolting cry of rage and despair: "May the day of my birth perish." Job laments the day of his birth and even curses the night of his conception. In other words, "Let these days be stricken forever from the record of human history!" cries the man traditionally praised for his patience.

In verse 8 Job calls upon the power of magicians and astrologers, "those who curse days" and control the movements of the sea monster Leviathan. Surely they can revenge this dreadful injustice!

❑ *Job 3:11-19.* If he could not escape being conceived, Job asks, then why couldn't he have died at birth? Or why couldn't he have been miscarried? He could have been spared the pain of life. In death, kings, slaves, prisoners, and infants who "never saw the light of day" all share the same restful fate.

THE TERRORS OF GOD **13**

❑ *Job 3:20-26.* Now Job turns and speaks directly to God. "Why are you doing this, God? Why do you allow those of us who suffer most to continue in our misery? Why not give us what we most desire—death? Instead, you make us hunt for it like buried treasure!" Job pleads with God to explain why God gives "light" (life) to those who are most wretched, the very ones God constrains. Job now morbidly feasts on his own sighs and groans. His worst fears have materialized, causing him constant turmoil and frustration.

❑ *Job 4:1-6.* Since Job has finally spoken, his friends now speak. Eliphaz, no doubt the senior member of the trio, begins by asking Job if he can tell him something without upsetting him. Without waiting for an answer, Eliphaz plunges in, unable to contain his distress over what he has just heard. "Remember, Job, what it was like when you were the strong and competent one, giving advice and consolation to the unfortunate! Now that the roles are reversed, why are you so impatient and distraught? Remember your religion, Job! Can't you rely on it when the going gets rough?"

❑ *Job 4:7-11.* Eliphaz next appeals to a time-honored tradition: "Who, being innocent, has ever perished?" Schooled in the doctrine of strict retribution, Eliphaz is confident that justice is always done. God's anger shrivels those who ask for trouble like a blast from a white-hot furnace. Sinners are like the ferocious lion that perishes for lack of prey. The implication, of course, is that Job must be guilty of wrongdoing.

❑ *Job 4:12-21.* Here Eliphaz claims the authority of a personal revelation. While in a deep sleep he experiences a moment of real terror and dread. A shadowy form glides by him and delivers the message that mortals cannot be righteous (vindicated) before God. Not even angels inspire God's confidence, much less mortals who live in bodies of clay. Easily uprooted, mortals die without ever discovering the meaning of life.

❑ *Job 5:1-7.* Feeling righteous anger, Eliphaz begins openly to taunt Job: "Call if you will, but who will answer you? To which of the holy ones will you turn?" In other words, once God has decided to punish someone, no lesser power can intervene. Eliphaz, a man of wisdom and experience, knows the inevitable outcome of foolishness or disobedience. Job's passionate outbursts show how unwise he is. All his anger will be the death of him. Eliphaz grants that the foolish do seem to "take root," but he himself has done something to thwart the fool's progress. He has called down curses on the fool's dwelling and on his children. When they seek justice at the city gate, no one will plead their cause. The fool's wealth is then enjoyed by others, but he has no one to thank but himself. "As surely as sparks fly upward," mortals are born to do mischief.

❑ *Job 5:8-16.* Eliphaz says he would confess his guilt and then throw himself on God's mercy—because despite our mistakes, God is merciful and just. God sends the rain. God elevates the humble, thwarts the evildoer, and saves the poor from oppression. God is the hope of all needy ones, the vindicator of all victims.

❑ *Job 5:17-27.* Finally, Eliphaz concludes his arguments by saying, "Job, you really ought to be glad all this is happening to you. God is disciplining you now; but if you take it like a man, God will reward you by restoring you to a happy and whole relationship with the world. You will be kept safe during famine and war. You will never need to fear slander or destruction. You will form a covenant with the stones of the earth and the beasts of the field so that your livestock and crops will be forever safe. You will have many children and live to a ripe old age. I know what I'm talking about! I'm telling you this for your own good."

❑ *Job 6:1-7.* Rather than answer his friend's arguments point by point, Job continues to rant about the enormity of his suffering. His misery is heavier than all the sands of the sea. But in fact his suffering is immeasurable, and this explains why he speaks so rashly. "God is a relentless hunter pursuing me," cries Job. "The poison on God's arrows seeps into my spirit, and I am terrified!" Why shouldn't Job complain bitterly? He is like the wild donkey who brays noisily when he has nothing to eat. Instead of good nourishment, Job is served tasteless and disgusting fare that he refuses to swallow—a reference, perhaps, to the kind of advice Eliphaz is dishing out.

❑ *Job 6:8-13.* Although Eliphaz has told Job that his religion should be a source of hope to him (4:6), Job still insists that his only desire is for God to let him die. No matter how painful

THE TERRORS OF GOD   **15** it might be, death would bring with it the consolation of knowing that he, Job, had at least remained faithful to God's commands. Job does not want to curse God; but he fears that should he have to suffer like this much longer, he would be in danger of blasphemy. How strong, how patient, does God expect Job to be? "I am powerless to help myself!" cries Job. "Any resource I might once have had to see me through this ordeal has been taken from me."

❑ *Job 6:14-23.* Job, unable to help himself, cannot rely on his friends either. Whoever refuses kindness to a friend, claims Job, forsakes true religion. Job's friends are as unreliable as the streams of Palestine that are flooded in the spring but give out in the heat of summer when they are needed most (verses 15-20). In the presence of unspeakable suffering, fear overwhelms friendship. Job begs his friends to explain their callous rejection of him. "Have I asked for anything from you?"

❑ *Job 6:24-30.* Despite Eliphaz's self-confident pronouncements, Job remains convinced of his own innocence. "Tell me precisely what I have done wrong!" he challenges. "If you speak truthfully, I can take it." But Job knows that Eliphaz's accusations are groundless. "What is it you are condemning in me?" he asks. "Is it my frantic ravings? What do you expect from someone in despair?"

Job accuses his friends of despicable, self-serving callousness. They are capable of casting lots over the weakest and most defenseless members of society, fatherless children. They would sell Job to the highest bidder. "Look me in the eye," says Job. "You know I won't lie to you. Change your mind (verse 29); and don't do me an injustice. My self-respect, good name, and future are at stake. Have I said anything untrue? Do you think I wouldn't know if I had done wrong?"

❑ *Job 7:1-6.* Human life in general, Job says, is like military conscription or forced labor. Job feels like a slave who longs for the working day to end or a hired servant waiting for wages. Days of fruitless labor lengthen into endless, empty months. Even his nights are plagued with insomnia. Yet Job is sure that this cannot continue for long. His body is virtually rotting away before his very eyes. Like the clacking of the weaver's shuttle, his days fly by as his life ends without hope.

❏ *Job 7:7-10.* Now Job directs his remarks to God. "Remember," he warns, "I am not long for this world; and while I will never live to see happiness again, neither will you, God, see me! For while you are watching me, I shall suddenly vanish, hidden forever from you." Once he descends to Sheol, Job will never be able to return; and no future vindication will be possible. If God does not act quickly to clear Job's name, it will be too late.

❏ *Job 7:11-21.* With nothing left to live for, Job sees no reason to restrain himself. He will say exactly what he thinks and express his true feelings. Job believes he is being hounded by God and persecuted in the most sadistic way possible. "Am I a sea monster that must be guarded constantly lest the forces of chaos overwhelm the world?" asks Job. "If I look for comfort in sleep, then you molest me with nightmares. I hate my life; being strangled to death is better than what I am putting up with now. God, leave me alone."

Job wonders why humans are so important to God that they must be tested night and day. Why, he wonders, is he God's target? "Even if I were a sinner, why not pardon me and be done with it?" Job asks. Yet Job takes some solace in the thought that he will escape God's malevolent gaze in the grave.

DIMENSION THREE:
WHAT DOES THE BIBLE MEAN TO ME?

As we begin to study the poetic dialogues in Job, we find our perspectives on the problem of innocent suffering and strict retribution are now governed by two opposing views—that of Job, the innocent sufferer, and that of his friends who offer counsel.

Job 7:16—Despair as the Experience of God's Enmity

"I despise my life," says Job (7:16). Everything has changed for him. He has lost his wealth and status, his family, his health, and his hope for the future. But Job is aware of an even greater loss: He has lost the friendship of God, who is now his enemy. This change in a once perfect relationship is absolutely inexplicable to Job. He knows he has not sinned, so why is he suffering? Since he can conceive of no other reason for his plight, Job concludes that God has suddenly initiated a cruel and perpetual surveillance of him. His former protector has now become the enemy.

Although drastically changed, Job's relationship to God continues. For Job still speaks to God and asks God to help him either by vindicating or killing him. But for Job, it is now essentially a relationship of enmity. Job's desire to blot out his past and dispense with any possible future is a direct attack on the wisdom and integrity of the Creator who brought his life into being, directed its course, and has plans for its future.

Reflect on the times in your life when you have been in despair. What external events contributed to your despair? How did despair color your view of your past? your future? How did despair affect your perception of your relationship to God? Did you hold God accountable for your misfortune? If not God, who or what did you believe was responsible for your suffering? Did God appear to be absent from you or indifferent in your time of despair, or did you feel persecuted by God? Did you reach the point where you longed for death? What kind of solution would death have provided? What eventually brought you out of your despair?

Job 4:1 – 5:27
Saying the Right Thing at the Wrong Time

Eliphaz opens his remarks to Job with the advice to have confidence in his religious traditions (4:3-6). He then proceeds to remind Job of all the truths they both have lived their lives by: The innocent never perish, but sinners get their just desserts; mortals cannot be righteous in the eyes of God but are instead born mischief-makers; honest confession will evoke a merciful response from God; and, finally, God's discipline should be seen as a blessing in disguise.

Most of us know from previous experience with the Scripture that these insights about the way God deals with humankind are affirmed over and over again in the Bible. We also know of times when these generalizations have accurately described or forcefully addressed a situation in our own lives.

18

Yet in Job's situation, these answers are wrong. Far from providing a solution to Job's dilemma, they add to his frustration.

Eliphaz, without any actual evidence of wrongdoing on Job's part, decides that because Job suffers, he must have sinned. His conclusion is erroneous, and his advice rests on a false assumption. Eliphaz is as ignorant as Job is of the reason for Job's suffering. The real reason transcends both conceptions of the freedom and justice of God. Thus, what is appropriate counsel in one context is bad advice in another.

Recall situations when you have been called upon to offer comfort and consolation. What were your assumptions about the causes of suffering? What evidence did you have for reaching your conclusions about the nature of the problem and its appropriate solution? Did you find yourself using any of Eliphaz's arguments? What other faith traditions did you call on? How well were your counsels received? Did you find yourself getting irritated when (and if) they were rejected?

Now recall a situation when you were offered consolation by a friend. What faith traditions were offered as explanations for your suffering or as solutions to it? Given the particular situation you faced, were they a source of real comfort or of further aggravation? Why?

Who can say to him,
"What are you doing?" (9:12).

—— 3 ——
Contending With God
Job 8–10

DIMENSION ONE:
WHAT DOES THE BIBLE SAY?

Answer these questions by reading Job 8

1. Whom does Bildad hold responsible for Job's plight? (8:4)

2. What does Bildad say God will do for Job? (8:6)

3. Where should Job look for help in understanding his plight? (8:8)

4. What is the fate of those who forget God? (8:13)

5. What follows the destruction of the godless? (8:18-19)

6. How does God treat the blameless? (8:20-22)

7. Why doesn't Job believe he can dispute with God? (9:3)

8. What are the marvelous things God does that Job finds impossible to understand? (9:5, 6, 7, 8, 9)

9. What else makes a challenge to God impossible? (9:11)

10. Why doesn't Job expect mercy from God? (9:13)

11. What is Job's only course of action? (9:15)

12. How does Job think God will respond to his summons? (9:16)

13. Why does Job believe this? (9:17-18)

14. Why doesn't Job believe he can defend himself in a contest with God? (9:20)

15. How does Job feel about God's justice? (9:22)

16. What does Job claim is God's response to the sudden death of innocent people? (9:23)

17. What does Job think might hapen if he tried to forget his troubles? (9:27-28)

18. What does Job think might happen if he tried to make himself acceptable to God? (9:30-31)

Answer these questions by reading Job 10

19. Why is Job willing to complain so freely? (10:1)

20. What questions would Job like to ask God?

_____ (10:2)

_____ (10:3)

_____ (10:4)

_____ (10:5)

_____ (10:9)

21. Why does Job think that God has created him? (10:12-14)

22. What happens if Job tries to assert himself? (10:16-17)

23. What does Job think he has a right to ask from God? (10:20)

DIMENSION TWO:
WHAT DOES THE BIBLE MEAN?

❏ *Job 8:1-7.* Unable to keep silent, another of Job's friends, Bildad, now joins the argument. He immediately accuses Job of speaking irresponsibly (verse 2). God does not act unjustly or do evil. The deaths of Job's children show that they must have sinned, yet Job need not suffer for their transgressions. Job only needs to turn to God in prayer (verse 5). If Job is indeed innocent, God will restore Job to his former state of health and prosperity—as if this is what Job were demanding. No matter how demeaning his present state of affairs may be, says Bildad, God can turn this disaster into a blessing (verse 7).

❏ *Job 8:8-10.* Bildad then advises Job to turn directly to the wisdom of the past and the traditions of his ancestors. Job will find an answer there.

❏ *Job 8:11-19.* Bildad shares this ancestral wisdom with Job in the form of proverbs. Our tradition teaches us, he says, that we must be rooted in God. Those who are not rooted in God are like the fragile papyrus that withers even before it has been cut down (verse 11-12). The godless have nothing on which to lean or rely. Like a feathery spider's web, their hope can support no weight at all (verses 14-15). Bildad compares the fate of the godless to that of a plant that thrives momentarily but, when destroyed, leaves no trace or memory (verse 18). So much for the joy of this kind of rootless existence. Where the godless once flourished, more and equally short-lived life springs out of the dust (verse 19).

❑ *Job 8:20-22.* Bildad believes, as does Eliphaz, that God will never abandon the innocent or aid the guilty. Bildad believes, and assures Job, that the innocent are eventually vindicated and that their enemies will suffer defeat.

❑ *Job 9:1-12.* "Yes, yes, I know all that!" says Job. "But how can I hope to vindicate myself before God? If I wanted to prove my case against God (as in a court of judgment), I would not be able to answer even one question in a thousand!" (verses 2-4). Job realizes that no one can defy God and be successful (verse 4). No one can ever understand the divine but violent God who first creates mountains and then overturns them. Can one trust a God who causes earthquakes? Can one call to account a force that darkens the heavenly bodies and subdues the waves of the seas? What hope does Job have if he chooses to wrestle with a God who can do these things, a God who first creates and then thinks nothing of destroying what has been created?

God, invisible and forever out of Job's reach, is free to come and go, turning Job's life upside down. No one can even utter a word of protest (verses 11-12).

❑ *Job 9:13-24.* Job knows that the God who crushes the allies of Rahab (an ancient sea monster like Leviathan) (verse 13) will have mercy on him. Job does not know what he would say if he could find and confront God. Though innocent, Job could only appeal for mercy in the presence of such power. Job is convinced that God would never listen to him anyway (verse 16).

Job does not hope for mercy because God has already judged and condemned him. Job absorbs blow after blow; but before he can get his balance, some fresh disaster strikes, leaving him breathless (verses 17-18). Job knows that in any contest with God, might will prevail over right (verse 19). Whatever words he might have the courage to say would be twisted by God so that Job would end up accusing himself (verse 20).

Job feels misery, rage, and despair. Convinced that the God who could vindicate him is determined to destroy him, Job accuses God of not having a system of justice. "It is all the same . . . 'He destroys both the blameless and the wicked.' " In fact, God laughs when sudden calamity overtakes the innocent. God stands by as the earth is delivered into the hands of the wicked and deliberately blinds those who administer justice (verses 23-24). This is the God his friends advise him to petition.

❏ *Job 9:25-35.* Job complains again about the brevity and meaninglessness of life. His days fly by as fast as a royal courier runs, like a papyrus boat skimming along the Nile, or like an eagle swooping down on its prey. He is so certain of condemnation that if he tries to make the best of things, he is still gripped with fear and anxiety (verses 27-29). If he tries to clean himself with the strongest possible cleansers, God responds by plunging him into a pit that makes him dirtier and filthy with guilt (verses 30-31).

If Job were fighting another human being, Job might have a chance of defeating him. An arbitrator or umpire would then be chosen to decide fairly who was in the right. Such a mediator would have the authority to compel the guilty party to make restitution. Job assumes that the mediator would decide in his favor and force God to stop terrorizing him (verses 33-34). But no one can judge God and compel God to do anything. Job must face God alone and undefended.

❏ *Job 10:1-7.* Job's total despair gives him a kind of desperate courage that others lack. He has nothing left to lose, so why not say exactly what he thinks? Even though Job is convinced he will never get his "day in court," he nevertheless knows exactly what he would say. "If I could call God to account," says Job, "here is what I would say." And then Job launches into a long series of questions: "Why are you fighting against me? Do you enjoy oppressing the work of your own hands (me)? Do you really know what it means to be human? Is your vision so limited, like that of my friends, that you must search for a reason to condemn me, even though you know I am innocent?"

❑ *Job 10:8-17.* Job reminds God that he, Job, is God's own creation (verses 8-9). Job then compares the seminal fluid of his father to milk that curdles in the womb (verse 10). This shapeless being is then clothed with skin and flesh and given structure by adding bones and sinews (verse 11). Thus Job is given the gift of life, and he affirms that he had always understood that gift of life to be evidence of God's unfailing love and care (verse 12).

Job now believes that in creating him God had a hidden purpose, a malicious intent. All this time God had actually been watching Job and waiting to condemn him whether he sinned or did not (verses 13-15). If Job dares proudly to assert his own integrity, God hunts him as though he were evil itself (a lion), renewing his attacks with fresh armies (forces) (verses 16-17).

❑ *Job 10:18-22.* Job returns to the theme of his original outburst (Job 3): "Why was I born?" (verses 18-19). Job knows his days are numbered. He wants God to leave him in peace for the little time he has left before descending forever to Sheol.

DIMENSION THREE:
WHAT DOES THE BIBLE MEAN TO ME?

Job 9:32-35—Calling God to Account

Both Bildad and Eliphaz advise Job to petition God for mercy. Job responds by asking, "How can I ask my accuser for mercy?" Job looks around and sees no evidence that God is merciful. Instead, he sees a universe torn by cosmic upheavals and human misery. He sees evidence of a God who is willful, cruel, and capricious. Job sees a God who long ago abandoned any pretense of being committed to justice, if indeed God ever had any such pretensions!

Someone, a powerful mediator, is needed to call God to account, to say, "What are you doing and why?" Of course, no such mediator exists; for no one has the authority to judge God or to require changes of God. Job knows, therefore, that when and if the time ever comes, he will have to speak for himself. In preparation for this possibility, Job has a list of questions he wishes to ask God. He would like nothing better than to say to God, "What are you doing?"

Place yourself in Job's position, and take a good look at the world you live in. What evidence do you see of God's creative power? of a power of destruction? Do you attribute that power of destruction to God? What conclusions do you draw from what you see? Does God care for the creation or not? Suppose you were given the opportunity to question God. What questions would you ask? What arguments would you make?

Job 8:8—Considering What the Fathers Have Found

Bildad is a conservative, a staunch supporter of the community's valued traditions. His perspective on human frailty and the limitations of individual experience ring true and carry weight, especially with those of us who have learned to value the wisdom of our elders. We know there is much to be said for consulting the past. A Bible study such as this one is an inquiry into "bygone ages." We recognize that the ancient traditions of our faith community still have the power to communicate to us today.

So what is wrong with Bildad's advice to consult the past? As with the advice of Eliphaz, we cannot consider what Bildad says apart from the total context of the Book of Job. The particular traditions Bildad consults, those of proverbial wisdom, are certainly true in a general sense. But they are not accurately applied to Job's situation of suffering. The broader and more general a truth, the harder it is to use in addressing a real, and complex, dilemma.

The reality of Job's experience is far more complex than proverbial wisdom can handle. Proverbial wisdom most often presents us with a God whose reactions are always predictable. Bildad's solution—It was your children who sinned, not you.— is just as inadequate a response as Eliphaz's conclusion that Job himself must have sinned. Job responds by saying, in effect, "Look around you, and you will see that God is thoroughly unpredictable. The reality of God is more marvelous and terrible than anything the fathers have ever been willing to admit!"

Reflect on the "truths" about God that you consider to be proverbial or axiomatic. Can you imagine a situation in which the truest of the truths you cling to would not be true at all? How would you respond in such a situation?

Though he slay me, yet will I hope in him;
I will surely defend my ways to his face (13:15).

—— 4 ——
The Cost of Vindication
Job 11–14

DIMENSION ONE:
WHAT DOES THE BIBLE SAY?

Answer these questions by reading Job 11

1. Does Zophar expect Job to be vindicated? (11:2)

2. Who is needed to set Job straight? (11:5-6)

3. Is Job getting what he deserves? (11:6)

4. What does Zophar ask Job? (11:7)

5. What is Zophar's advice to Job? (11:13-14)

6. What will happen if Job follows Zophar's advice? (11:15-16)

7. What may Job expect if he fails to follow Zophar's advice? (11:20)

Answer these questions by reading Job 12

8. How does Job respond to Zophar's advice? (12:3)

9. What has Job become to his friends? (12:4)

10. How do the comfortable treat the unfortunate? (12:5)

11. Who or what will testify to the truth of what Job says? (12:7-9)

12. How does God exercise wisdom and might? (12:13-15) (To answer, summarize in one or two sentences the nature of the activity described in verses 14-25.)

Answer these questions by reading Job 13

13. Whom does Job really wish to address? (13:3)

14. What would be the wisest thing for Job's friends to do? (13:5)

15. What does Job accuse his friends of doing? (13:7-8)

16. How will God treat Job's friends if they show partiality? (13:10-11)

17. What is Job willing to risk for the chance to defend himself? (13:14-15)

18. What does Job ask God to do? (13:20-21)

Answer these questions by reading Job 14

19. Why shouldn't God pass judgment on mortals? (14:1-3)

20. Why is there more hope for trees than for humans? (14:7-12)

21. What does Job wish God would do? (14:13-17)

22. What is the grim reality Job knows he must face? (14:18-19)

DIMENSION TWO:
WHAT DOES THE BIBLE MEAN?

❏ *Job 11:1-6.* The third friend, Zophar, is by now quite exasperated with Job. Zophar accuses him of speaking boastful, self-vindicating babble. Job is being scandalous to allow this shocking nonsense to continue. In fact, Zophar is just as anxious as Job to have God respond to this situation. Zophar believes that were God to be revealed to Job, Job would see that he had indeed sinned and was actually receiving less punishment than he deserved.

❏ *Job 11:7-12.* Zophar questions Job with pointed sarcasm: "Can you, a mere mortal, claim to understand the deep mysteries of God? Can you measure the Almighty?" Zophar strains for a way to describe the strangeness and immensity of God. It is higher, deeper, longer, and broader than the dimensions of all creation (verses 7-11). How can anyone question God's right to inflict punishment where and when God pleases? God knows what evil is and will deal with it accordingly (verse 11). Someone as witless as Job appears to be cannot be expected to understand these things.

❏ *Job 11:13-20.* Zophar has no new explanations or solutions to offer. Like Eliphaz and Bildad, he advises Job to repent and beg God for mercy. If Job is wise enough to do this, he can look forward to a safe and secure life. The misery, dread, and anger he is now experiencing will be forgotten; and he will once again be looked up to by others. But if Job continues to be foolish, he will find that his only solution will be death.

❏ *Job 12:1-6.* "Of course you know it all," mocks Job. "When you die, all wisdom will die with you!" But Job knows as much as Zophar; he was taught the same things. Job, and not Zophar, has become the laughingstock to everyone. Job accuses his comfortable friends of callous contempt for his suffering.

Meanwhile, the unscrupulous, "who carry their god in their hands" (who trust in their own power), rest secure.

❑ *Job 12:7-12.* Job calls on the rest of creation to verify what he says: "Ask the animals; they'll tell you! They all know about the power and so-called justice of God. Every living thing exists at the mercy of God (verses 7-10). Look around you! Listen! Then you will know that what I am saying is true."

❑ *Job 12:13-25.* "God may be wise," says Job, "but God is also powerful. What God chooses to tear down, no one can hope to rebuild. What God wants to thwart, no one can bring to pass" (verses 13, 14). Job goes on to catalogue the fates of those who exercise power in human institutions: kings and their counselors, priests and princes, and even entire nations. The strongest of the strong are stripped of their defenses and left to grope blindly through chaos and confusion when God turns against them (verse 25).

❑ *Job 13:1-12.* Job then tells Zophar that they both know what the world is really like. Job feels he is wasting his time arguing with the likes of Zophar. He wants to argue his case before God. Frustrated at his inability to confront God, Job lashes out at his friends, accusing them of trying to whitewash the reality of God's cruelty and injustice with partiality and lies. If they were truly wise, they would keep silent (verse 5). But they try to gain favor with God by defending God's treatment of Job at the cost of telling the truth. Job warns them that this double-dealing on their part will work against them when God chooses to judge them (verses 9, 10). Their advice promises much but is useless (verse 12).

❑ *Job 13:13-28.* Job is now ready to challenge God—even at the risk of losing his life in the process. Job has no hope and feels certain that God will destroy him for this act of arrogance. And for the first time during his ordeal, he admits that maybe he is not so innocent.

But God does not call Job. Job does not understand why he had been abandoned by God (verse 24). He is desperately trying to find an answer and decides that God is holding the sins of Job's youth against him (verse 26). After being ignored, Job accuses God of making a public spectacle of him and branding his feet like a slave.

❏ *Job 14:1-6.* Job again returns to feelings of despair. God's continual harassment of insignificant creatures is hard to understand (verse 3). Having set severe limits on human life, God should leave mortals alone so they can enjoy their lives.

❏ *Job 14:7-17.* Ironically, a tree has more hope of life and regeneration than do humans. An apparently dead tree stump may yet sprout new life, but human death is devastatingly final (verse 12). Contemplating this absurdity, Job wonders why after his death his stay in Sheol cannot be temporary. He only wants to die until God's anger has passed (verse 13). Job would be glad to wait in Sheol for God to call him back to a life freed from God's terrible wrath. Job imagines some future time when God would not simply forget his sins (whatever they may be) but actually "seal them up" so they are hidden forever (verse 17).

❏ *Job 14:18-22.* Of course, this freedom could never happen. Job believes his own destruction to be as inevitable as the erosion of the earth by water. God always wins; mortals are the real losers. In the grave nothing can be known or anticipated except the ceaseless torment of personal pain (verse 22).

DIMENSION THREE:
WHAT DOES THE BIBLE MEAN TO ME?

Personal Vindication and the Desire for Immortality

Job is in a terrible dilemma. Falsely accused, his only hope of acquittal is a face-to-face confrontation with his accuser—an encounter that he is certain will result in his death. Yet he is willing to take this terrible risk. Why?

Job has lost everything except his life and the conviction of his own innocence; and of the two of these things, he values the latter far more than his life. We have seen in Job's response to Zophar that he bitterly resented being made a public laughingstock. This would be true of anyone, but public humiliation was an especially terrible form of torment in Eastern cultures. There a higher value was placed on "saving face" than on life itself. Job appears to be no exception to this general rule. He is willing to risk certain death for the chance to clear his good name. Why is Job willing to pay such a terrible price for personal vindication? To understand just how vital an issue personal vindication was for Job, we need to recognize how closely linked this issue is to the human desire for immortality.

Ancient Israelites did not believe in a bodily resurrection or any kind of afterlife until shortly before the New Testament period. For centuries, Sheol was all Israelites could look forward to. Although Sheol did not mean total extinction, it was not a place of life in any true sense of the word.

Instead of looking forward to bodily resurrection or the continued existence of an immortal soul, the Israelites looked to a kind of immortality in the memories of the living. The memory of a good person was treasured and kept alive by that person's descendants. Since Job's children were all dead, even this hope was denied him. The living who will remember Job will remember him as fallen, sick, despised, and very angry. They are certain to conclude, as have the three friends, that Job must have done something terribly wrong to merit such treatment at the hands of God. Believing, as he must, that this life is the only life, Job has a great deal at stake in clearing his name. He will give his last breath for the sake of the only kind of immortality it is possible for him to conceive of: honor and fidelity.

Most Christians are not aware of the extent to which their belief in an afterlife affects their hopes and values, as well as their actual behavior. Try putting yourself in Job's place. If you were certain that the only life left to you was the days between today and the day of your death, how would your thinking and behavior change? On what things would you place the highest value? How would you alter the way you spend your time or your other resources? Would you treat other people differently? How would your expectations about children and other family members be affected? Would this change of belief change your relationship to God in any way? Under these circumstances, is there anything for which you would be willing to risk the rest of your life? If so, what?

But you even undermine piety
and hinder devotion to God (15:4).

—— 5 ——
Scandalous Suffering
Job 15–17

DIMENSION ONE:
WHAT DOES THE BIBLE SAY:

Answer these questions by reading Job 15

1. What does Eliphaz accuse Job of doing? (15:4-11)

2. How does Eliphaz attempt to explain Job's rebellion against God? (15:14)

3. On what does Eliphaz base his advice to Job? (15:17-18)

4. According to Eliphaz, what fate awaits the wicked? (15:20-24)

5. Why is this the fate of the wicked? (15:25-26)

6. What warning does Eliphaz issue to the wicked? (15:31)

Answer these questions by reading Job 16

7. What kind of comforters are Job's friends? (16:2)

8. Job claims that he too could speak like his friends. Why doesn't he? (16:6)

9. Job renews his complaints against God. What are they?

_____ (16:7)

_____ (16:9)

_____ (16:11)

_____ (16:12)

_____ (16:13)

10. What is Job's response to this violent treatment? (16:15-17)

11. Who will vouch for Job? (16:19)

12. What does Job ask God to do for him? (17:3)

13. What are the consequences of God's treatment of Job?

_____ (17:6)

_____ (17:7)

_____ (17:11)

_____ (17:15-16)

DIMENSION TWO:
WHAT DOES THE BIBLE MEAN?

❏ *Job 15:1-6.* Eliphaz speaks to Job a second time, but without any of the polite preliminaries. He says no self-respecting wise man would babble on as foolishly as Job. Job's words are now more than simply unprofitable, claims Eliphaz. Job is being subversive! The *Contemporary English Version* translates verse 4 as, "Your words are enough to make others turn from God and lead them to doubt."[1] Job's ravings against God are not only offensive to the believer. They actually threaten to undermine faith in God. Therefore Job's rebellious words are a crime. No matter what he may or may not have done in the past, Job stands condemned by his own blasphemous words.

❏ *Job 15:7-16.* Eliphaz sarcastically challenges Job to explain the source of his wisdom. "Were you the first human being created?" he asks. "Were you there to see how God made the world at the beginning of time? Maybe you listened in when the heavenly court was convened! What makes you think you know so much?" sneers Eliphaz.

Eliphaz wants to know why Job is rejecting the consolations of God and the gentle words of his friends. Obviously, Eliphaz has been hurt by Job's harsh rejection of his words of comfort and advice. He does not understand how Job can be so rebellious and say such things. Verse 13 is evidently a rhetorical question, since Eliphaz immediately answers himself: Mortals born of unclean woman are corrupt and untrustworthy. If angels are not trusted, can God trust humans who drink evil as effortlessly as if it were water (verses 14-16)?

❑ *Job 15:17-35.* But Eliphaz is not quite ready to give up on Job. Eliphaz is sure that if he can just get Job to listen, he will succeed in wringing a confession from him. Once again he reminds Job that he, Eliphaz, speaks from experience (verse 17). All he says is verified by the authentic and orthodox teachings of the Wisdom tradition (verses 18-19).

Eliphaz now launches into a long and graphic description of what happens to the wicked. Whether he intends to explain Job's pitiful condition or to scare him into submission is not entirely clear. The wicked suffer constantly, Eliphaz claims. Wrongdoers live with the ceaseless torment of a guilty conscience and the ever-present fear of divine reprisal. Nothing they do can protect them from retribution.

The cause of this intense personal anguish is rebellion against God (verse 25). The wicked foolishly assail God, protecting themselves with human devices such as shields and fat (or prosperity). Brazenly, the wicked inhabit cities that have been destroyed and are now under a curse (verses 25-28). Yet, this immense effort to defy the Almighty is sheer illusion. The wicked will not endure and neither will their wealth. "Trusting what is worthless . . . [they] will get nothing in return" (verse 31).

❑ *Job 16:1-5.* Eliphaz's renewed efforts to reach Job do not achieve the desired effect. Tired and offended, Job calls Eliphaz and the others "miserable comforters." Why does Eliphaz go on and on? Job feels he could argue a case as well as Eliphaz. He could assemble the quotes, cite experiences, and edify Eliphaz as well as Eliphaz edifies him.

❑ *Job 16:6-17.* But why should Job bother to argue his case? How would it help the sufferer to manipulate words? If he speaks, it does nothing to relieve his pain; and if he is silent, the result is the same. Nothing helps. Job blames his miseries on the hostility of a God he had once worshiped so faithfully. Perversely, this same God has shriveled Job up in the heat of his wrath.

Exhausted, bitter, and totally defeated, Job sees himself torn from limb to limb, a public disgrace victimized by a remorseless hunter (God) and sadistic mobs (verses 8-11). He sees himself broken, slashed, skewered, and assaulted like a defenseless city (verses 12-14). Even though he is utterly innocent of all wrongdoing, Job has done penance by sewing himself into sackcloth, covering himself with dust, and weeping endlessly (verses 16-17).

❏ *Job 16:18–17:2.* Job cries out to the earth for vengeance: "Do not cover my blood." That is, "Let the whole world see the crime that God has perpetrated against me! Let my cry for justice be heard and not silenced."

Even now, Job bravely affirms, there is a witness in heaven who will speak up for him in the divine assembly, just as neighbor testifies on behalf of neighbor (verses 19-21). But Job's brave words are always followed by the darkest despair. Recognizing how hopeless this dream of vindication really is, Job reminds himself that his days are short and that, indeed, his spirit has been shattered by God's enmity. He cannot ignore, and perhaps he cannot really disbelieve, the mockers who surround and torment him for sins he cannot identify.

❏ *Job 17:3-5.* Who will speak for Job? His friends? They are the first to accuse him. The mysterious witness in heaven? Job knows that no one can compel God to do justice. Who will risk himself on Job's behalf? No one. Only God knows that Job is innocent, so Job appeals once more to God. "Take a risk for me: Lay down a pledge on my behalf. No one else will! You have closed their minds against me. You know they are wrong. These friends are traitors who would inform against me. May the eyes of their children fail!"

❏ *Job 17:6-16.* Job continues to stress the horrors of public humiliation. This seems to be what aggravates him most. Now a symbol of the worst of human degradation, Job is spat upon by passersby (verse 6). The righteous are appalled at what they see. What ghastly sin could account for such a vile and repulsive state of affairs? The innocent stand fast, however. They grow in strength and are not wasted by the fiery blast of God's wrath (verses 8-9).

Job taunts his friends to come at him again. He knows that none of them is really wise. His life is at an end, and his plans for the future are shattered. Job no longer cares what kind of nonsense they may say, whether it be that night is really day or that the light is almost darkness (verses 10-12). Again, Job feels despair and hopelessness; for nothing awaits him but the pit of Sheol and the "worm" of death and decay. Will hope descend with Job into the grave? He knows it will not.

DIMENSION THREE:
WHAT DOES THE BIBLE MEAN TO ME?

Job 17:6-10—-Public Suffering

Throughout the dialogues, we notice that Job is perpetually irked by the public nature of his suffering. Suffering the tragic and devastating loss of children and property is bad enough. But why must these losses be emblazoned as diseased sores all over his body? These hideous symbols of distress shout a message to everyone who passes by: "This man is a sinner! Just imagine what this man must have done to merit such a ghastly fate! This man deserves what he has gotten!" Job understands fully that his misfortunes rise up to testify against him. (See 16:8.) He has been forced by the sheer weight of his misery to play the part of the penitent, even though he has done nothing that requires this response.

The Bible records many instances of human suffering, but the most powerful of these accounts all have one important feature in common. They describe a kind of suffering that is all the more terrible because of its public nature. The accounts of the Crucifixion in the Gospels describe the death of Jesus as a public execution accompanied by humiliating gestures and contemptuous treatment on the part of the executioners. (See Mark 15:16-20, 29-32.) The humiliation of Jesus is similar in kind to that described by the psalmist (Psalm 22:6-8, 16-18). It was soon compared by the early church to the public suffering of the "servant of God" whom everyone assumed had been "stricken by God, / smitten by him, and afflicted." (See Isaiah 53:4.)

Most people can recall the experience of feeling unjustly punished and publicly humiliated at some point. But it is difficult for us to grasp how such an experience would assault the integrity (and the very existence) of the Oriental male. Loss of face is still, in some parts of the East, considered worse than dying. Public humiliation or scandal sometimes precipitates suicide. When the Accuser deals Job misfortune after misfortune and finally afflicts him with disease, he has made sure that Job will become the object of public judgment and scorn. Job is not allowed to sulk in secret or to waste away in private sorrow and despair. Rather, his torment becomes a form of public entertainment. Everyone is free to watch his misery and to draw the obvious conclusion.

Today public suffering is more public than ever with advances in mass media. As you read the daily paper or watch the news on television, how many people are held up for public scrutiny, either because they are the victims of disaster or the center of some scandal? What kind of information is presented about these figures? What sort of visual images do the printed and electronic media select to entice readers and viewers? What conclusions do you find yourself reaching about the causes of public suffering as a result of what you see and read? Do you find yourself passing judgment on people who would appear to have brought suffering on themselves? Do you feel any pleasure or satisfaction in watching someone receive "poetic justice"? Since personal suffering is becoming public, what is the most appropriate public response?

Job 15:1-6—Doing Away With the Fear of God

Eliphaz makes it clear to Job that he has joined the ranks of the scandalized public. Job's ferocious accusations against God are not simply the words of a miserable mourner. They constitute a real threat to faith and piety. Think back to what Job has said about God. God deliberately allows those who long for death to linger in their pain (Job 3:20-23). God has pursued Job with arrows dipped in poison (Job 6:4). God terrifies Job and sets a ceaseless watch over him (Job 6:14-19; 7:18; 9:18). God is sadistic enough to laugh when the innocent suffer calamity (Job 9:23). God delights in unleashing the forces of chaos and bringing the successful of this world to their knees in defeat (Job 12:13-25). And finally, Job has as much as called God a vicious murderer (Job 16:9-18). Is it any wonder, then, that Eliphaz and all the rest of us feel threatened by this kind of rage and rebellion?

Hearing God spoken of in such terms is upsetting. Can we analyze why Job's response to suffering is as threatening as it is? In the first place, we all wish to worship a just and loving God. Job's accusations, if true, place Eliphaz in the position of either having to join Job in condemning God or of totally abandoning his ideas about the nature of God. Eliphaz would then have to admit that God is not just as humans understand the word and that God's universe is disorderly and unpredictable. Eliphaz assumes the only other possible explanation for Job's plight. Job is in the wrong, and his suffering is a manifestation of God's predictable justice. This conclusion affirms Eliphaz's interpretation of his own experience as well as the tradition in which he has been instructed.

Religion is above all else an attempt to find meaning in life. So Job's contention that there is no justice is clearly an assault on any religion that insists on the justice of God. If Job is right, and he seems so sure that he is, then Eliphaz must go through some painful readjustments. The explanations that have offered him security and reassurance in the past will have to be modified or abandoned in the face of new evidence. How anxious are persons to undergo the painful process of having to reconstruct a system of meaning after their cherished beliefs have been blown apart?

Take time to reflect on what seems most threatening to your religious beliefs or world view. Is your faith threatened more by what people say or by what people do? Or is your faith threatened most by actual events you have experienced or witnessed? Does anything pose as grave a threat to your faith as the image of an unjust God or the problem of innocent suffering? Is there any single attribute of God—such as justice, love, mercy, power, or predictability—on which your faith hinges?

Religious beliefs provide a system of meaning and order in an otherwise disorderly world. Do your religious beliefs provide you with a means for surviving disorder? Or do they require an orderly world for their maintenance? Do you, like Job's friends, search constantly for an acceptable explanation of suffering? Or do your religious beliefs allow you to live without acceptable explanations? How would you respond to the charge that the God you worship is a capricious, vicious, and sadistic tyrant?

---

[1] From the *Contemporary English Version*; Copyright © American Bible Society 1991.

I know that my Redeemer lives
(19:25).

—— 6 ——

Harsh Realities and the Claims of Faith
Job 18–19

DIMENSION ONE:
WHAT DOES THE BIBLE SAY?

Answer these questions by reading Job 18

1. According to Bildad, what does Job think of his friends? (18:3)

2. Does Bildad expect Job's anger to change anything? (18:4)

3. What causes the downfall of the wicked? (18:7)

4. According to Bildad, what terrors pursue the wicked? (18:12, 13, 14, 17, 19)

5. What is the reaction of all who witness this fate? (18:20)

Answer these questions by reading Job 19

6. What effect do the friends' words have on Job? (19:2)

7. If Job has sinned, whose concern should that be? (19:4)

8. Who, insists Job, is really responsible for his suffering? (19:6)

9. What response does Job get to his cry for justice? (19:7)

10. How does Job describe God's actions? (19:11-12)

11. How do the members of Job's household and his closest friends now treat him? (19:13-19)

12. What does Job really want from his friends? (19:21)

13. What do his friends do instead? (19:22)

14. What is Job's hope? (19:23-24)

15. Why is this Job's hope? (19:25-26)

16. What will Job's Redeemer enable him to do? (19:26-27)

17. What should Job's friends expect if they continue to blame him for his problems? (19:28-29)

DIMENSION TWO: WHAT DOES THE BIBLE MEAN?

❏ *Job 18:1-4.* Now it is Bildad's turn to speak again. Like Eliphaz, he is impatient with Job's long speeches and loud complaints. "How long is this going to go on, Job? It's time for you to listen and for us to speak!" And, like Eliphaz, Bildad is insulted by what he has heard. Job seems to think they are all as witless as cattle. What difference will all these histrionics finally make? He wants to know if Job would destroy the whole earth just to be vindicated.

❏ *Job 18:5-14.* Bildad is certainly not the most original of the three friends. He can think of nothing better to say than to elaborate further on the fate of the wicked, much as Eliphaz has already done. (See Job 15:17-35.) But Bildad adds his own special twist to his counsel. It is true, he says, that the wicked suffer horribly; but their suffering is actually self-inflicted. The wicked fall into their own traps, the traps they have set for others. Bildad's theory is that evil actions come back to affect the evildoer. He then lists every device he can think of for entrapment: schemes, nets, traps, snares, and ropes.

Surrounded by their own instruments of ruin, the wicked face terrors that torment them physically and terrify them with visions of oblivion. Specifically, these terrors take the form of the loss of strength, calamity, a terrible disease or plague (the first-born of death), and the devastating loss of the basis of confidence (verse 14). Finally, the hapless evildoer is dragged before the "king of terrors," or death itself (verse 14).

❏ *Job 18:15-21.* Now the ungodly one faces a fate that is even worse than death: the loss of progeny and the destruction of his memory among the living. Verses 15-19 describe ultimate oblivion. No trace of the wrongdoer will remain. In place of children and possessions, there will be brimstone (sulfur to disinfect his house) in his tent (verse 15). Like a plant without moisture, he will shrivel and die, barren and fruitless. No survivors will honor his memory or carry on the family line. Virtually everyone ("men of the west" and "men of the east") will witness his ghastly demise. They will be horrified at the destruction they see.

❏ *Job 19:1-6.* Job knows that Bildad is describing Job's fate. No vague generalizations these! His friends are throwing words at him like bricks. Time after time they assault him without shame or remorse (verses 2-3). "If it is true that I have gone astray," says Job, "my error remains my concern alone." Is Job admitting to sin here? Probably not. Rather, he seems to suggest that if he had sinned, his sin would be his own problem and not the concern of his friends. After all, they have not been injured by his so-called transgressions.

Job's friends wrong him deeply when they assume that his terrible suffering is proof of personal guilt. "Hear this!" fumes Job. "It is God who is responsible for my suffering. It is God, and not I, who has set the trap that now ensnares me." (See verses 5-6.)

❏ *Job 19:7-12.* Caught in God's net, Job cries, "Murder!" "Help!" His only answer is silence and the conviction that there is indeed no justice (verse 7). Job continues his lament with another list of complaints. God has hemmed him in, plunged him into darkness, stripped him of honor, and assaulted him on every side. God has, in effect, killed Job ("I am gone") and destroyed his last hope. Like a military commander, God has positioned troops around Job's tent where they maintain a vigilant watch (verse 12).

❏ *Job 19:13-19.* Job returns to the problem of public humili-ation and its worst consequence: rejection by family and friends. Previously, Job complained of the cruel taunts of passersby. Now he confesses to a far more painful ordeal. The members of his own household, his wife and relatives, guests, and even his servants, find him repulsive. Hideous in his suffering, Job finds himself alienating those he loves and ignored by those who previously came at the snap of a finger. Little children torment Job, and his closest and dearest friends now despise him. Job faces universal rejection at the time of his greatest need (verse 19).

❏ *Job 19:20-22.* Job's claim to have escaped "with only the skin of my teeth" (verse 20), or "by the skin of my teeth," has become a saying in the English language. We sometimes use this phrase to describe a narrow escape. Yet biblical scholars concede that they really do not know precisely what is meant by this vivid image. What is clear is that Job hopes to sway his friends to pity. He does this by drawing attention to his pitiful physical condition. Brokenhearted, Job begs his friends for a merciful word. He wants to know why they join God's pursuit. To "get enough of my flesh" is to say to "eat the flesh of someone," which is a Near Eastern way of saying slander. So Job wants to know why they are not satisfied with the way they have been slandering him.

❏ *Job 19:23-25.* "If only my words could be written down!" cries Job. "If only they could be written in a book or engraved permanently in rock!" Job is again responding to the threat of total extinction. He has no children left, no friends or relatives who will vouch for his innocence. If his words of self-defense could be preserved beyond his own death (as in a book), then he would feel assured of eventual vindication (verses 23-24).

❏ *Job 19:26-27.* Even now Job is sure that a redeemer or vindicator will finally appear and stand up for him (as in a court of law) to testify on his behalf. Job does not think this final vindication will occur before his death. Yet death itself cannot thwart Job's ultimate acquittal. For despite all evidence to the contrary, Job clings to his original vision of an orderly world where justice prevails. Thus he is hopeful that he will see God and that God will be on his side.

HARSH REALITIES AND THE CLAIMS OF FAITH　　　**49**

The Hebrew in verses 26-27 is difficult to translate. To see just how difficult, consult the chart that appears below and on page 51 that illustrates the various ways popular versions of the Bible translate this controversial passage. Read each version and then answer the questions that appear below the versions.

Job 19:25-27

New Revised Standard Version

For I know that my Redeemer
    lives,
        and that at last he will stand
        upon the earth;
and after my skin has been thus
    destroyed,
        then in my flesh I shall see
        God,
whom I shall see on my side,
    and my eyes shall behold,
        and not another.

King James Version

For I know that my redeemer
liveth, and that he shall stand at
the latter day upon the earth;
    And though after my skin
worms destroy this body, yet in
my flesh shall I see God;
    Whom I shall see for myself,
and mine eyes shall behold, and
not another.

*Good News Bible, The Bible
in Today's English Version*

But I know there is someone in
    heaven
        who will come at last to my
        defense.
Even after my skin is eaten by
    disease,
        while still in this body I will
        see God.
I will see him with my own eyes,
    and he will not be a stranger.[1]

The Bible: A New Translation,
by James Moffatt

Still, I know One to champion
        me at last,
            to stand up for me upon
            earth.
This body may break up, but
        even then
            my life shall have a sight of
            God;
my heart is pining as I yearn
        to see him on my side,
            see him estranged no longer.[2]

---

[1] From the *Good News Bible, The Bible in Today's English Version*—Old Testament: Copyright © American Bible Society 1976: New Testament Copyright © American Bible Society 1966, 1971, 1976. Used by permission.

[2] From the Holy Bible, translated by James Moffatt (Harper and Row, Publishers); used by permission.

The Revised English Bible	The New Jerusalem Bible

But I know that my
    vindicator lives
and that he will rise last to
    speak in court;
I shall discern my witness
    standing at my side
and see my defending counsel,
    even God himself,
whom I shall see with my own
    eyes,
I myself and no other.[3]

I know that I have a living
    Defender
    and that he will rise up last,
        on the dust of the earth.
After my awakening, he will set me
    close to him,
    and from my flesh I shall look
        on God.
He whom I shall see will take my
    part;
    My eyes will be gazing
        on no stranger.[4]

[3] From *The Revised English Bible.* Copyright © 1989 Oxford University Press and Cambridge University Press.

[4] Excerpts from *The New Jerusalem , Bible,* © 1966, 1985, by Darton, Longman and Todd, Ltd., and Doubleday and Company, Inc. Used by permission of the publisher.

Examine the versions above to see if there is any consensus on the following issues:

1. Which versions imply that Job expects to be vindicated after death? Do any versions suggest otherwise?
2. Are the versions unanimous in stating that, alive or dead, Job will see God while still in the flesh?
3. Does the passage identify the redeemer? Which versions imply that it is God, and what device(s) do they use to show this? Do any versions leave open the possibility that the redeemer might be someone else?

Because the ancient manuscripts available to scholars do not agree among themselves, there is confusion as to whether Job believes he will be vindicated before or after his death and whether Job will see God with or without his flesh. Finally, there has always been much speculation as to the identity of Job's redeemer. Is it God, as some of the versions seem to imply? How consistent would this be with the position Job has taken in the dialogues that God is his accuser?

❑ *Job 19:28-29.* Job seems unable to sustain this rare flash of hope. But momentarily bolstered, he lashes out at his accusers. "If you persist in condemning me," he warns, "be afraid of the sword; for you will be judged."

DIMENSION THREE:
WHAT DOES THE BIBLE MEAN TO ME?

Job 9:25-27—My Redeemer Lives

Job 19:25-27 is one of the most famous and familiar passages in all Scripture. We have heard this passionate affirmation of vindication many times. We know that these lines are thought to epitomize radical faith. How many of us would recognize these words as coming from the mouth of Job? Consider your previous experiences with this passage. In what setting(s) have you encountered it? What have you always assumed that this passage meant?

Now look again at the chart. How do the different translations affect your understanding of the passage's meaning? Does looking at this passage in the total context of the poetic dialogues give you a different perspective on it? How? What do these differences suggest to you about interpreting biblical material apart from its literary context?

Jot down your own working definition of the word *redeemer.* Is your definition an exclusively theological one? Now consult a good dictionary to see what the word means when it is used in a secular context. Several key passages in the Old Testament describe the role of a redeemer in ancient Israel. See Leviticus 15:23-24, 47-55; Numbers 35:19; Deuteronomy 25:5-10. Take time to study these references to see how they might apply to Job's situation. Which, if any, seem directly related to Job? What light do these passages shed on why Jesus might have been called a redeemer? In what ways does the Christian's view of Jesus' role as redeemer differ from what Job calls for? Are you in need of the kind of redemption Job seeks?

To understand the importance of Job 19:25-27 as a statement of radical hope and faith, we must know what was at stake from Job's point of view. This necessitates reading the passage from a pre-Christian perspective. Job and his contemporaries believed that beyond death, there was nothing to hope for except a semi-existence in Sheol. They also believed that God is predictably just. Obedience to God is rewarded in this life with the blessings of wealth, health, and progeny. Disobedience brings physical suffering and social humiliation. Now consider Job's experience. Does it square with what he has been taught to believe is true?

A clear conflict exists between traditional teaching and Job's experience on the issue of God's justice and the predictability of retribution in this life. What happens when there is such an obvious tension between religious belief and experience? How do our experiences force us to modify or even to abandon our beliefs? What does Job appear to be doing here? Is he changing or abandoning his religious beliefs? If so, what changes are made or at least hinted at? Does anything in the dialogues suggest that Job is willing to reinterpret his experience to preserve his original beliefs about the justice of God?

Most commentators would agree that Job 19:25-27 is the strongest affirmation of faith in the Book of Job. What is the source of Job's faith in ultimate vindication? Is it his original belief in the justice and goodness of God? Or would it be more accurate to say that what Job has faith in is his own innocence?

Think back to faith-testing experiences in your own life. What happened when the realities of your experience did not square with what you had been taught to believe? Have the faith stands you have made rested on what you have been taught or on previous experiences or both?

— 7 —

God's Justice and Ours
Job 20–21

DIMENSION ONE:
WHAT DOES THE BIBLE SAY?

Answer these questions by reading Job 20

1. Does Zophar listen to Job's complaints? (20:2)

2. How do Job's remarks make Zophar feel? (20:3)

3. What does Zophar tell Job? (20:5)

4. To what does Zophar compare the life of the sinner? (20:7)

5. When will the godless perish? (20:11)

6. What happens to the riches of the wicked? (20:15)

7. What will happen to the fruit of the wicked person's toil? (20:18)

8. Why is the wicked person punished? (20:19-20)

9. What will God do to the wicked? (20:23)

10. What are God's weapons? (20:24)

11. What will reveal the iniquity of the godless? (20:27)

Answer these questions by reading Job 21

12. What kind of consolation does Job want? (21:2)

13. When may Job's friends mock him? (21:3)

14. How should Job's friends respond to his plight? (21:5)

15. What question haunts Job? (21:7)

16. According to Job's observations, what is the fate of the wicked? (21:8, 9, 10, 13)

17. What is the attitude of the wicked toward God? (21:14)

18. Why is this their attitude? (21:15)

19. Does Job think the children of the wicked should suffer for their parents' sins? (21:19-20)

20. Why does Job feel this way? (21:21)

21. Can Job explain this injustice? (21:22)

22. What is the common fate of rich and poor? (21:23-26)

23. What are Job's friends thinking? (21:27-28)

24. Where should Job's friends seek confirmation of his words? (21:29)

25. What is the testimony of travelers? (21:30-33)

26. What do Job's friends offer him for comfort? (21:34)

DIMENSION TWO:
WHAT DOES THE BIBLE MEAN?

❑ *Job 20:1-6.* Now Zophar gets a second chance with Job. Insulted and extremely agitated, he has been busy mentally formulating answers while the others have been speaking. "Don't you get the point, Job?" he asks. "From the beginning of time the truth has been self-evident and cannot be challenged: The joy of the wicked is short lived!"

❑ *Job 20:6-11.* To illustrate, Zophar explains that the arrogant, excessive ambition of the godless merits them nothing. In the end, they share the fate of their own excrement. (Zophar is the coarsest of the three friends.) The wicked die at the height of their power and vanish without a trace. The children the godless leave behind will be reduced to such dire straits that they will be forced to beg from the poor.

❑ *Job 20:12-19.* Zophar makes the point that everything the wicked devour in their greed turns to poison in their stomachs and must be disgorged. What has been stolen from the poor is like a sweet-tasting delicacy, hidden under the tongue to prolong enjoyment. When the delicacy is finally swallowed, it becomes as fatal as a serpent's venom. Then the wicked are forced (by a predictably just God) to vomit it back up again (verse 15). Visions of plenty will elude the wicked. Ironically, every plundered treasure must be returned before it can be enjoyed. Every gain the godless labor over is ultimately lost to them.

❑ *Job 20:20-26.* The cause of this misery is insatiable greed. Devouring everything in sight, the gluttonous become victims of a fatal indigestion (verses 21-22). Zophar gleefully pictures the wicked tormented by a bellyful of divine wrath. Then a meal of judgment will rain down on the victim from above. Finally, skewered by a shaft of lightning ("the gleaming point"), the wicked flee in terror only to be consumed by the fire of God (verses 23-26).

❑ *Job 21:1-5.* Job once again appeals to his friends to listen carefully. After they have listened to him, then they may sneer. He reminds them that his complaint is not against them, or any mortal, and that he has good reason to rant. Job informs his friends that they should indeed be horrified, not at what they hear (namely, his angry words), but at what they see (the sight of an innocent man broken by God's anger).

❑ *Job 21:7-16.* All three of Job's friends have argued that the wicked suffer dearly for their sins. Now Job responds by telling them that the evidence he and others have seen belies their simple explanations. "The wicked do thrive," claims Job; and he wants to know why. Prosperous and secure, they live to a ripe old age and enjoy the satisfaction of seeing their children launched into the world successfully (verse 8). They are surrounded by peace and plenty and even enjoy a quick and painless death. But these blessings, claims Job, have nothing to do with the fear of God. Rejecting religious practices as profitless, the wicked are responsible for their own successes (verses 15-16). Ironically, those who reject God outright fare better than those who strive to be faithful!

❑ *Job 21:17-26.* Job continues his argument from the evidence. "How often (Be honest!) is the life of the wicked extinguished? Do the wicked really suffer from their own sins? Does God really inflict physical pain on the sinner as punishment?"

Both Zophar (Job 20:10) and Eliphaz (Job 5:4) have argued that the sinner's children are punished as well. Job cites this tradition (Job 21:19), only to condemn it. "Let them suffer for their own sins!" he fumes. "Let them live to experience God's fearful justice" (verses 19, 20). Job knows that once in Sheol, the sinner does not know or care about the fate of his offspring. So where is the justice in that? But who can tell God what to do? Job's friends may say what they please. The fact is that the prosperous sinner and the hapless, innocent sufferer share the same fate. Once dead, both the wicked and the righteous are merely a feast for worms (verses 23-26).

❑ *Job 21:27-34.* Stung by the rebuke of his friends, Job snarls at them, "I know what you're thinking! All this talk about the wicked is really directed at me. What's happened to my house? Hasn't it been destroyed? And what's happened to my children? Haven't they been victimized for my so-called sins?" (verses 27-28).

"If you don't believe me," Job challenges them, "ask the people who have really been around. Ask the ones who travel, and see if you won't accept their testimony!" Job is sure that the tales of world travelers will bear him out (verse 29). They have seen that the wicked are indeed safe from God and that no one has either the nerve or the will to confront and punish them. Even when they die, the wicked receive honor and are kept secure (verses 32-33).

DIMENSION THREE:
WHAT DOES THE BIBLE MEAN TO ME?

In this section of Job we are presented with two problems: (1) the fact that the wicked often seem to prosper and (2) the injustice of the claim that children must suffer for the sins of their parents. To prepare for class discussion, read the arguments on these issues found in Chapter 18 of Ezekiel.

Job 21:7—Why Do the Wicked Live?

Job's question, meant to challenge Zophar, is a question that all of us have asked at one time or another. It is the other side of Job's original question—Why do the innocent suffer? Both questions are troublesome, yet one is more troublesome than the other. Both questions are raised in the Scripture, yet only one of them is directly addressed. Which of these two questions is more troublesome to you? If you are like most

GOD'S JUSTICE AND OURS   **59** people, you are probably bothered more by the suffering of the innocent than by the prosperity of the wicked. Not surprisingly, this is the question the Scripture addresses more directly.

As we have seen, Job raises this question, as does Jeremiah (Jeremiah 12:1-2) and the psalmist (Psalm 73:3-12 and 94:1-7). But it is important to recognize that although the Bible raises the question, it does not attempt to answer it. Instead, Scripture is concerned with the fact of this apparent injustice (It acknowledges that the wicked do thrive.) and the need to help the righteous deal with their frustration.

Reflect on what you already know about the witness of the Scripture to the problem of evil. The wisdom tradition teaches that sinful actions contain the seeds of their own destruction, with an emphasis on punishment in this life. Israel's prophets foretold a decisive and terrifying "Day of the Lord" when not just individuals but entire nations would suffer as a consequence of their wickedness. (See Amos 5:18-24; Malachi 3:13–4:3.) Jesus also speaks of a time of judgment when people will be judged on the basis of actions they themselves would have considered inconsequential (Matthew 25:31-46). The books of Daniel and Revelation describe a holocaust when the forces of evil will be defeated once and for all.

To say, however, that evil must and will be defeated does not necessarily make it any easier to cope with. The wisdom psalms (for example, 37:1-9 and 73:1-2, 10-26) recognize this problem and offer advice to the frustrated. How sound or helpful do you think this advice is? What has been your method of coping with the evidence that evil is permitted to flourish? Where do you look for consolation?

Notice that in Ezekiel 18 the concern shifts from punishment to rehabilitation of the sinner. The prophet assures us that God has "no pleasure in the death of anyone," including sinners (Ezekiel 18:32). In fact, Ezekiel's words sound very much like those of Jesus, who taught that the conversion of the sinner is more precious to God than the continued faithfulness of the righteous. (See Luke 15:3-7.) Does this statement seem just? This passage from Ezekiel calls a human sense of justice into question. How often do we unthinkingly apply our own sense of justice as a standard by which to judge God? How often do we measure ourselves by what we know of God's justice as it is revealed in the life and teachings of Jesus?

Job 21:19—God Stores up Their Iniquity for Their Sons

The belief in collective justice (when one sins, all suffer) is an ancient one. In one form or another this notion permeates the Scripture, including the New Testament. Consider, for example, Paul's understanding of the church as the body of Christ that suffers when a single member is injured (1 Corinthians 12:26).

One of the starkest expressions of collective justice appears in the belief that the generations of a single family must suffer for each other's sins, either the children for the sins of the parents or vice versa. (See Exodus 20:5.) According to Job, this is another of life's great injustices. Study Ezekiel's argument against this belief (Ezekiel 18:1-20). Whose sense of justice, says the prophet, is outraged by this demand? Whose sense of justice appears satisfied with this arrangement?

Reflect on what you have learned about individual responsibility and collective guilt from your own experience. What generally happens to the children of parents who lead reprehensible lives? Do the children suffer? What about the reverse situation? How are parents affected when their children live outside of the law? What word of hope do you find in Ezekiel 18 for persons in this situation?

If only I knew where to find him
(23:3).

—— 8 ——
The Hidden God
Job 22–24

DIMENSION ONE:
WHAT DOES THE BIBLE SAY?

Answer these questions by reading Job 22

1. According to Eliphaz, who profits when people live wisely? (22:2)

2. Why is Job being punished? (22:4-5)

3. Of what serious sins is Job supposed to be guilty? (22:6, 7, 9)

4. What are the consequences of Job's sinful acts? (22:10)

5. Why does Job feel free to sin? (22:12-14)

6. What advice does Eliphaz give Job? (22:21-25)

7. How will God respond to this change in Job? (22:27)

Answer these questions by reading Job 23

8. What is Job's greatest frustration? (23:3)

9. If Job could find God, what would he do? (23:4-5)

10. How would God respond to Job's plea? (23:6-7)

11. Why is Job still confident of vindication? (23:11-12)

12. What is it about God that continues to frighten Job?
    (23:13-14)

Answer these questions by reading Job 24

13. What does God not reveal to those who know and serve
    the Almighty? (24:1)

14. Whom would Job like to see judged? (24:2-4)

15. What happens to the victims of those who exploit the poor? (24:5-11)

16. How does God respond to the prayers of the poor? (24:12)

17. Who rebels against the light? (24:14-16)

18. On whom do the wicked prey? (24:21)

19. What finally happens to the wicked? (24:24)

DIMENSION TWO:
WHAT DOES THE BIBLE MEAN?

❑ *Job 22:1-5.* Eliphaz begins the third round of the dialogues by citing yet another axiom: "Can a man be of benefit to God?" In other words, is there anything humans do that benefits God in any way? Eliphaz is making the point that the wisdom of the wise and the obedience of the righteous benefit them, not God. Eliphaz is also convinced that while human righteousness gives God no particular pleasure, human wickedness is not something God can ignore. Since God does not punish anyone for being righteous, the only possible explanation for Job's tragic circumstances is that Job is a sinner.

❑ *Job 22:6-11.* This accusation is followed by a catalogue of Job's sins. This so-called blameless man is obviously guilty of gross injustice. He is also guilty of callousness toward the poor. He has without justification taken their clothing in pledge and left them naked to the elements (verse 6). Further, Job has refused to give food and water to those who need them (verse 7). He has appropriated land unfairly (verse 8) and refused charity to widows and orphans (verse 9). Only sins this evil could account for the drastic treatment Job is receiving. Predictably, Job is experiencing the terrors Bildad had described earlier. (See Job 18:8-11.)

❑ *Job 22:12-20.* Eliphaz goes on to accuse Job of deviousness and indifference. Apparently, Job feels that because God is so far removed from creation, God is actually unaware of what happens on earth. So Job is free to do as he pleases (verses 12-14). Ironically, this is the opposite of what Job has claimed. Job really believes that God constantly watches him. (See Job 7:17-20.)

Eliphaz warns Job against clinging to the old way of the wicked (verse 15). If Job continues to be obstinate, he can expect to be cut off in his prime, just as it appears he will be. As others have done before him, Job has rebelled against God. He assumed that the Almighty did not know about his sins and was powerless to intervene. Job is strengthened in this conviction because (for a while at least) he did indeed prosper (verse 18). But once judgment strikes, as Job has been struck, the righteous rejoice and heap scorn on the sufferer (verse 20).

❑ *Job 22:21-30.* Eliphaz concludes his third and last discourse by advising Job to stop fighting it, "submit to God," and acknowledge defeat. Then he will find peace and prosperity (verse 21). Eliphaz outlines a set of conditions that will ensure success. First, Job must return to God in humility. Then, Job must remove all traces of unrighteousness from his household (verse 23). Finally, Job must renounce his love of worldly wealth and make God alone his treasure (verse 25). This purging of Job's greed and pride will make him worthy in God's eyes. All Job's prayers will be heard and answered. Whatever decisions he makes or tasks he undertakes will bear fruit (verses 27-28). Job can never hope to see himself vindicated because he is too proud. Eliphaz claims humility and innocence are the only way to salvation.

❏ *Job 23:1-7.* Job does not respond to Eliphaz's diatribe. He returns instead to his own obsessions. Bitter and frustrated, Job realizes that the confrontation with God he so desperately desires is impossible. Still, Job fantasizes about what he would do, what he would say, should the opportunity arise. Job literally burns with the desire to plead his case. He wants to say what he must say and, in return, hear what God would say. So sure is Job of his innocence that he can claim that God can and must listen to him. A righteous man such as Job can face God without fear of being overwhelmed and be sure of a fair hearing (verses 6-7).

❏ *Job 23:8-10.* But God is nowhere to be found. In vain, Job seeks everywhere for God (verse 8-9). Although Job cannot find God, he is nonetheless convinced that God knows where he is. God is aware of everything that happens to Job. Sooner or later Job's innocence will shine forth, just as gold emerges from the smelter's furnace (verse 10).

❏ *Job 23:11-17.* In an effort to reassure himself, Job carefully recounts his efforts to be faithful (verses 12-13). Yet even these memories do not offer him the comfort he seeks, for Job knows that God never changes. In other words, God cannot be swayed. What God wants for Job, God will see to it Job gets, whether it be condemnation or vindication (verses 13-14). Realizing this, Job has no hope of persuading God to see things differently. He is actually frightened by the thought of God's presence. How can he ever hope to find justice, hemmed in as he is by darkness, pain, and despair (verses 15-17)?

❏ *Job 24:1-17.* Job returns now to questions about the justice of God. Everyone talks about the time of judgment, but who has ever witnessed it? When, really, will the wicked be punished? And why are God's faithful ones forbidden the satisfaction of seeing justice dispensed (verse 1)?

Meanwhile, evil is everywhere, but especially in the lives of the poor who are so easily exploited. Here Job lists sins that are committed against the poor. The poor have to put up with unscrupulous people who alter boundaries and steal livestock (verse 2). They rob the widows and orphans of their means of livelihood and force them to scavenge for a living like beasts in the wilderness (verses 3-5). Naked and unsheltered, the poor are forced to glean in the fields of the wicked and to work for wealthy landlords who refuse to share their bounty (verses 6, 10-11). Some cruel creditors will even snatch a widow's child to sell into slavery as a pledge against her debts (verse 9). Appalling as these conditions are, God remains distant and removed; and the pitiful prayers of the dying and wounded go unheard (verse 12).

Job's list of divine injustices seems to get longer and longer. Next he lists a whole class of sinners who "rebel against the light." These sinners rely instead on darkness, stealth, and deception. Job is outraged at the success of murderers (verse 14), adulterers (verse 15), and thieves who "break into houses" to reach their prey (verse 16). Operating only at night, these malefactors remain safely sealed indoors during daylight hours.

❏ *Job 24:18-20.* Here Job quotes the arguments of his friends. His friends have claimed that the wicked are as insubstantial as the scum carried away on the surface of a stream. The holdings of the wicked remain sterile and fruitless (verse 18). The sinners will disappear like evaporating water, forgotten in the places where they once rose to power and prominence (verses 19-20).

❏ *Job 24:21-25.* Job continues in a cynical vein. Sinners who "prey on" barren women seem to prosper. Just when they think they are at the point of death, God raises them up and actually prolongs their lives so that they may live to exploit another victim. Yet finally, these too wither and fade.

DIMENSION THREE:
WHAT DOES THE BIBLE MEAN?

Job 23:2—Where Can We Find God?

The God of Scripture is a paradoxical God. God promises to be with the people, but that presence is not something we can feel with our senses. Nor is it something we can verify to the satisfaction of anyone else. Much of the time the God who promises to be with us and for us seems utterly absent.

Often God seems absent when our need for divine solace is greatest. Job felt close to God in times of prosperity. But his sense of God being with and for him evaporated; and the absent God became the angry, hostile God. Frustrated and hurt, Job is sure things could be set right if only God would listen to him. To his dismay, Job discovers that God cannot be summoned. Apparently, Job has tried all the standard methods of approach. But his efforts have brought no results. In desperation Job has hurled insults at the Almighty to provoke a response, but the silence simply absorbs Job's curses.

Reflect on the times in your life when you have felt abandoned by God. Does God seem farthest away when you are faced with suffering? with a difficult ethical decision? during a time of boredom? What has been your response to God's absence? Are you generally angry and depressed like Job? Does the absence of God leave you feeling that there really is no God? Was Job ever tempted to believe that?

Now consider the times when you have felt God's presence. How have these times differed in quality and context from the times when God seemed absent? Did you feel God's presence through a particular event or as a consequence of prayer? What do experiences of God's presence reveal about the divine identity and intent? What do they conceal?

Job 22:21—Agree With God and Be at Peace

Job's friends are convinced that the next step ought to be Job's. Eliphaz in particular harps on the need for Job to put things right with God. Review the conditions for and fruits of repentance set forth by Eliphaz in Job 22:21-28. We know that the assumption underlying this advice—that Job needs to repent—is false. But suppose it were not. Do you think Eliphaz accurately lays out what is involved in the process of repentance?

Now compare Eliphaz's advice with that of John to those who came seeking baptism from him. (See Luke 3:7-14.) Are they talking about the same kind of experience? What does John say are the fruits of repentance? What does Eliphaz promise will be the result if Job humbles himself? Is the repentance John preaches a way of summoning God to return to a right relationship with those who repent? Or is it a response to a summons by God?

Have you ever been advised to repent? If so, what were you taught about appropriate expressions of repentance? What were you told would be the results or fruits of your repentance? How did experience bear out the reliability of this advice? What kinds of experiences actually drove you to a state of repentance? What changes in living followed your change of heart? Did your act of repentance appear to "sway" God or induce God to "return" to you? Eliphaz promised Job that if he repented, he would once again be a powerful and effective figure. Does John make similar promises? Does Jesus?

But where can wisdom be found?
Where does understanding dwell? (28:12).

— 9 —

The Search for Wisdom
Job 25–28

DIMENSION ONE:
WHAT DOES THE BIBLE SAY?

Answer this question by reading Job 25

1. According to Bildad, what is the status of human beings before God? (25:4, 6)

Answer these questions by reading Job 26

2. Does Job appear pleased with the help he is getting? (26:2-3)

3. Can the dead in Sheol escape God? (26:6)

4. Of how much of God's power are mortals aware? (26:14)

Answer these questions by reading Job 27

5. How long will Job defend his integrity? (27:5)

6. What is Job's wish for his enemy? (27:7-8)

7. What will happen to the wicked? (27:14-17, 20, 21)

Answer these questions by reading Job 28

8. What do persons search for under the earth? (28:1-2)

9. How do miners descend into the earth? (28:4)

10. What else does the earth yield? (28:6)

11. Can any animal follow humans into the depths of the earth? (28:7-8)

12. What must be done to find treasure? (28:9-11)

13. Can humans find the place of wisdom as easily as they locate precious minerals? (28:12-13)

14. How much does wisdom cost? (28:15-19)

15. Where is the place of wisdom? (28:21)

16. Who alone understands how to find wisdom? (28:23)

17. What has God revealed about wisdom? (28:28)

DIMENSION TWO:
WHAT DOES THE BIBLE MEAN?

❏ *Job 25:1-6.* Bildad's third speech, unlike his others, is short. The rest of it is probably either missing or has been misplaced. It opens with a statement praising God's power and dominion over the entire universe. God can quell disturbances anywhere in the cosmos with a vast army of heavenly beings (verses 2-3). How, then, can any mortal hope to be righteous in the eyes of such overwhelming majesty? If the brilliance of the sun and moon is mere tarnish in the eyes of God, how much less must humans seem? "Compare yourself to a maggot or a worm, Job" (verses 5-6).

❏ *Job 26:1-4.* In a very sarcastic tone of voice, Job marvels at the help he is getting from his friends. Just look at what they have done for someone who does not have a single resource to his name. Think of the solace and support they have offered him in time of crisis. Job wonders who could possibly have sustained and inspired them as they set about the task of counseling such a fool as he.

❑ *Job 26:5-14.* Many scholars consider these verses to be the missing part of Bildad's speech. The tone and content of these verses (which focus on the orderly application of God's power in the universe) do not sound like anything else Job has had to say about God. Certainly, these verses do not logically follow Job's sarcasm.

Again, the point of these verses is to demonstrate the enormous scope of God's power. Sheol, or Abaddon ("The Place of Destruction"), was thought to be out of God's reach. Yet here the claim is made that not even Sheol provides shelter from God's eye (verses 5-6).

God can pitch the heavens as if they were a huge tent over the formless void where the earth will be. The chaotic waters are captured and contained in gigantic clouds that scurry across the face of the moon (verses 7-9). God draws the circle of the horizon and then sets limits for light and dark (verse 10). God causes the mountains to tremble. God also causes the sea monster Rahab to stop churning the sea (verses 11-12). Yet all these stupendous feats give only a hint of God's actual power (verse 14).

❑ *Job 27:1-6.* Job continues his response to Bildad with a solemn and angry oath: "As surely as God lives . . . " he swears. Note that the God who has betrayed and embittered Job is still a God Job can swear by. "For as long as I live," promises Job, "I will speak the truth only. Never will I concede that the three of you are right. Never will I concede that God punishes me justly for the sake of some sin!" Once and for all, Job makes it clear that his conscience is clear (verse 6).

❑ *Job 27:7-23.* Here Job curses his enemy: May he be treated as God treats the wicked. Yet who is Job's enemy? Hasn't he clearly identified God as the enemy? If so, then surely Job has passed the fine line that separates the ravings of a desperate man from real blasphemy.

Some scholars, however, believe that from verse 7 to the end of the chapter we have another displaced passage. This passage is perhaps the missing third speech of Zophar. This would resolve the difficulties we would otherwise have in trying to reconcile the message of these verses with Job's earlier speech about what happens to the wicked. (See Job 21.) The arguments in this passage, another diatribe against the wicked, sound old and stale. Nothing new is added except perhaps the point (in verses 16-17) that the righteous will profit from the worldly wealth of the wicked. Would you expect Job to argue this kind of a case? Would Job, whose family was destroyed by a whirlwind, predict the same kind of demise for the wicked (verses 21-23)?

❏ *Job 28.* Chapter 28, placed here as part of Job's response to Bildad, is actually an independent poem or wisdom hymn inserted into the dialogue. Although these are among the most skillfully written lines in the entire Old Testament, the poem still seems isolated from its surrounding context.

❏ *Job 28:1-11.* The poem opens with a description of the dangerous search people make for precious minerals deep in the earth. Despite the risks involved, miners open shafts into the mountainsides and descend on ropes, lamps in hand, to find treasures (verses 3-4). The poet contrasts the peaceful earth's surface where nourishing grains are grown to the seething cauldron below where the metals are forged (verse 5). And who but a creature created in God's image would attempt such a feat? No other creature would try such a difficult and daring enterprise (verses 7-8). Indeed, what beast could cut channels through rock or move a mountain?

❏ *Job 28:12-18.* But another task and treasure transcends even these. Hard as it is to find gold and sapphires, it is even harder to find wisdom. Mortals are at a loss to know even where to begin to look for it. Wisdom cannot be mined, much less purchased (verse 15). Wisdom is so precious that not all the gold of Ophir (a country where gold is plentiful) could equal its worth (verses 16-17). But, where is wisdom? This question haunts all creatures. No living thing can see its dwelling place. Even death knows of wisdom only by hearsay (verse 22).

The place of wisdom is known only to God. God alone can see into every corner of creation. In the very process of creating the universe, God discovered wisdom. Then God carefully examined and tested it (verse 27). Since God alone knows the place and nature of wisdom, only God can reveal these mysteries to baffled mortals. "Fear me," says the Lord. "Obey my commandments and turn away from evil. This is as much of wisdom as you need to know" (verse 28).

DIMENSION THREE:
WHAT DOES THE BIBLE MEAN TO ME?

Job 28:12—Where Shall Wisdom Be Found?

Many things distinguish humans from other living creatures. But certainly one of the most distinctive differences is the human's driving desire to learn, discover, invent, achieve, and acquire. The poet who wrote Job 28 was amazed at the verve and technical expertise of those who risked their lives to search for precious metals. Today, we are equally amazed by people who venture into outer space. Throughout history the human mind has applied itself to overcoming great obstacles. Sometimes this attempt is for personal gain, sometimes for the common good. But it is always in response to difficult challenges that pique curiosity without destroying either hope or initiative.

Philosophers and theologians are quick to remind us that our understanding of the meaning of life and God's will for the world lags far behind our technological advances. We spend huge sums of money and countless hours of effort to develop space age weaponry. But our ability to solve personal and international conflicts remains at an infantile stage of development.

Job 28, a real gem of the wisdom tradition, calls us to reflect carefully on our values and our quests. The poet knows how to measure human commitment to a difficult venture. How hard and for how long will we work at the task? How much patience and ingenuity will we invest in the search? How many risks are we prepared to take to achieve our goal? Will we let obstacles (such as mountains) stand in the way of our success?

Take a moment to identify what you think society in general values most highly. For what treasures will our country spend vast sums of money, divert resources of time, energy, and intelligence? For what ventures do we willingly risk the lives of our citizens? Now apply these same questions to the church and to yourself. Using the key indicators of time, money, energy, and intelligence, what would you say your faith community truly values? Where do you invest your scarce and precious resources? For what treasure might you willingly risk everything you have?

The wisdom tradition is unanimous in affirming that the most priceless treasure of all is wisdom itself. "For wisdom is more precious than rubies, / and nothing you desire can compare with her" (Proverbs 8:11). In much the same way, the New Testament tells us that where our treasures are, there will our hearts be also (Matthew 6:21). Jesus' parable about the pearl of great value exhorts us to risk all for the sake of a single goal. (See Matthew 13:46.)

What could we ever pursue with such single-minded devotion? What is wisdom that we should make it the most important thing in our lives? And doesn't the poet say that no matter how hard we look, we shall never find it?

We have seen by reading Job that the wise person is one who faithfully obeys God's commands and scrupulously avoids evil. Job himself was as wise as it was humanly possible to be. But this kind of wisdom, to which humans should certainly aspire, is not particularly mysterious, nor is it hidden. Through the conditions of the covenant, God has made plain what "fear of the Lord" really means.

In Job 28 we are introduced to a different dimension of wisdom, one that is indeed mysterious, elusive, and impossible to find. This poem is one of several passages (see also Proverbs 4:7-12; 8:1-36; 9:1-6) that personify wisdom. Specifically, these passages speak of wisdom as female. "Lady Wisdom," as she is sometimes called by Bible scholars, represents far more than the fear of the Lord. She is mysteriously bound up with the nature of the universe and the divine principles that govern it. In Job 28:27 God discovers wisdom while in the very act of controlling the elements and ordering the cosmos. She, Wisdom, is the pattern, the measure, and the means of God's creation. She is the answer to the question that everyone eventually asks: Why is the world the way it is? And for that very reason, she constantly eludes our grasp.

Job, who has always understood wisdom in terms of the fear of the Lord, is shattered when the rules no longer seem to apply. Lady Wisdom could supply the answer for him, but she is as unreachable as God. Yet it is a comfort to realize that the search for meaning does not begin and end with Job. And the search, though apparently endless, is certainly not futile. The early church recognized that the search for wisdom was full of surprises as well as fraught with risk and difficulty. What the world calls wise, says Paul, God labels mere foolishness. For the place where the wisdom of God is to be found is precisely the place where Jesus the Christ hung nailed to a cross. (See 1 Corinthians 1:20-24.)

I sign now my defense—
let the Almighty answer me (31:35).

— 10 —
Playing the Last Card
Job 29–31

DIMENSION ONE:
WHAT DOES THE BIBLE SAY?

Answer these questions by reading Job 29

1. What was life like for Job when God watched over him? (29:3, 8-10)

2. Why was Job so highly honored and praised? (29:12-17)

3. What did Job expect? (29:18)

4. How did people respond to Job's words? (29:21-23)

5. To whom does Job compare his former position in society? (29:25)

Answer these questions by reading Job 30

6. What type of people now mock Job? (30:8-9)

7. How do these people treat Job? (30:10, 13)

8. How has this affected Job? (30:16-17)

9. What has been God's part in Job's suffering? (30:18-21, 23)

10. How did Job treat others who suffered cruelly? (30:25)

11. Has Job received in kind what he has given others? (30:26)

12. How would God punish Job if he looked lustfully at a virgin? (31:1-3)

13. What would happen if Job told lies? (31:5-6)

14. When would another eat what Job sows? (31:7-8)

15. What would happen if Job committed adultery? (31:9-10)

16. Why would Job have to answer before God? (31:13-14)

17. What sins would cause Job to suffer a broken arm and shoulder? (31:16, 19, 21, 22)

18. What sins would result in punishment by the judges? (31:24-28)

19. Why would thorns grow instead of wheat? (31:38-40)

20. Whom does Job want to hear him? (31:35)

21. What would Job do with his adversary's indictment? (31:36)

DIMENSION TWO:
WHAT DOES THE BIBLE MEAN?

❏ *Job 29:1-10.* Just as the dialogues began with a heart-rending lament (Job 3), so now they end. Job is through speaking with his friends. He no longer looks for anything from them. In Chapters 29–31, Job empties himself of every last word of protest and defense. God the Judge is his audience, and the justice of God is his last hope.

Job begins his lament by reminding God of what their relationship had once been like. Before, God shed light on every path Job trod, so that the doubts and fears of ordinary folk did not worry him. Job enjoyed the blessings of a large family (verse 5), wealth (verse 6), and respect (verse 11). Job's judgments were requested and revered by everyone. Even chieftains and elders listened intently to Job (verses 8-10).

❏ *Job 29:12-20.* Yet Job's remarkable success was nothing accidental. Job, it seems, still shares the assumptions of his friends that virtue should ensure happiness in this life. He recounts his good works as if to account for these successes. The poor, especially widows, orphans, and those with handicapping conditions (verse 15), enjoyed Job's protection and passion for justice. Job also took up the cause of strangers and worked against oppression (verse 17). Job fully expected to die, after a long and happy life, surrounded by his children and their offspring (verse 18).

❏ *Job 29:21-25.* Job relishes his memories of exercising power and influence. A respected teacher of wisdom, Job's words were always the last words on any subject (verse 22). Those who sought his support found their spirits lifted by his smile. Without a murmur, they held his advice as binding as a king's command (verse 25).

❏ *Job 30:1-8.* A grim study in contrasts, Job has fallen from the height of social success to become an outcast. The sons of men Job would have once scorned to employ in the most menial jobs now jest at Job's expense. Those who mock Job represent the lowest elements of society. These violent young men have been ostracized by respectable people and are destitute. They have been driven beyond the gates of the city to scrounge for food and scraps. Sleeping in gullies, they huddle together and burn the roots of desert shrubs for warmth (verse 3-6).

❏ *Job 30:9-18.* In his misery Job has become a comforting symbol to this worthless riffraff. "Look at Job! Now even we have somebody to despise!" Since Job's condition speaks so clearly of God's rejection of him, those who have suffered human rejection are glad to find themselves no longer on the bottom. All the pent-up rage they have against society is unleashed in its full fury against Job (verse 11).

Although Job had devoted himself to defending the helpless, no one now steps forward to protect Job from these vicious attacks (verse 13). Like an unstoppable force, they have no compassion or common decency. Like stones from a breached wall, they roll recklessly on, causing chaos and injury wherever they go (verse 14). Job is helpless to stop them. He is tormented by his own vulnerability and the loss of his reputation (verse 15). His days are full of terrifying threats, and his nights are an endless round of pain and torment. Pain has wrapped itself around him like a garment (verse 18). But Job does not blame his misery on those hopeless wretches. Job knows that God caused it.

❏ *Job 30:19-23.* Devastated because God deserted him, Job accuses God of not giving him a fair hearing. "You ignore my cries for help; you pay no attention to my case!" Job, whose words were once listened to, suddenly finds himself at the mercy of forces he cannot control. Like a brittle leaf, he is tossed about in a storm of pain that he knows will end in certain death (verse 23).

❏ *Job 30:24-31.* Here Job appeals to God's sense of justice—a justice he has come to believe is warped. Job reminds God that he (Job) was always compassionate towards others (verse 25). Yet now that Job himself needs help (verse 24), evil comes in place of the good he expected (verse 26). The injustice of the situation infuriates Job so that he is "blackened, but not by the sun" (the NRSV translates this as "I go about in sunless gloom"), with rage and frustration (verse 28). Like the jackal and the ostrich, beasts known for their bleak and plaintive cries, Job sings now only of death and despair (verses 29-31).

❏ *Job 31.* Earlier Job refused his wife's advice to "curse God and die." (See Job 2:9.) But now Job is finally ready to force God's hand. He does this by uttering a string of oaths that will force God to respond. If these oaths, known as oaths of innocence, are in any way false, then God is obligated to ensure that the consequences threatened in the oaths are carried out. Silence or a refusal to act on God's part would signal Job's innocence. As you read through these oaths, take note of whether the punishments Job calls for seem to fit the crime.

❏ *Job 31:1-8.* Job begins with an implicit oath clearing himself of ever having lusted after virgins. "Ruin," he says, would be the certain outcome of such philandering (verse 3). Next, Job formally swears he is innocent of lying and deceit. He is willing to be weighed in a balanced pair of scales to test the truth of what he says (verses 5-6). Job also claims an honesty of intent: If he has ever coveted that which is not his, then may another reap what he has sown (verse 8).

❏ *Job 31:9-15.* Job swears he has never even been tempted to commit adultery. He would see his own wife "grind another man's grain" (become another man's concubine) rather than "lurk at [his] neighbor's door" (verses 9-10).

Job continues by swearing that he has always listened to the complaints of his slaves. Since slaves had few rights, this marks Job as an unusually compassionate man. Job knows that, whether master or slave, all people were created by God. He fears that should he neglect the needs of the powerless, he will be harshly questioned by God (verse 14).

❑ *Job 31:16-23.* Job takes special pride in his reputation as a defender of the poor and oppressed. He has defended widows and orphans and shared his worldly goods with them. Job has even opened his home to orphans and reared them with the love of a father (verses 17-18). Job would sooner see his arm broken than raise that arm against one of society's wretched ones. Job knows that the wrath of God is reserved for those who do not show mercy to the powerless (verses 22-23).

❑ *Job 31:24-28.* Job now portrays himself as a strict monotheist. He has put his trust in God, not in gold. He has never taken credit for earning his wealth. He knows it comes as a blessing from God. Job did not worship other gods, like the sun or moon (verses 26-27).

❑ *Job 31:29-34.* Job has never cheered when an enemy was ruined. He has never cursed those who wish to harm him. Job's doors have always been open and his tables full for travelers seeking safety from the dangers of the night (verses 31-32). In short, Job has no sins to conceal, no fear of intimidating crowds. Surely this is what it means to have walked in God's light. (See Job 29:3.)

❑ *Job 31:35-37.* This passage says it all. If a life like this does not speak so that God will hear, then what will? Job, in taking these oaths, has seized the initiative. He is determined to argue his case, even if his opponent never shows up in court. "Indict me if you can!" he roars. "And what wouldn't I give to see that indictment! What sins could possibly be written there?" With a final burst of glorious confidence, Job promises to wear the indictment (that cannot possibly contain anything incriminating) as proudly as if it were a crown. Then he will stride boldly to meet God.

❑ *Job 31:38-40.* Chapter 31 concludes with two final oaths, almost certainly misplaced here. Just as Job knows that no person can honestly bring a complaint against him, neither can the land. The land was known to "cry out" against injustices. (See Genesis 4:10 and Jeremiah 12:4.) Never has Job exploited peasant farmers for personal gain. Should he be lying, let him harvest a crop of thorns and weeds.

DIMENSION THREE:
WHAT DOES THE BIBLE MEAN TO ME?

Job 31:35—Playing the Last Card

In the experience of each person, there comes a time when every human resource has been exhausted. We have tried everything and stretched our hopes to the breaking point, when we realize that there is nothing left we can do. The next step is up to God.

Most of us resist reaching this point. Job certainly does. But seeing it coming, he is driven to one final act of desperation. At the absolute end of his tether, Job decides to take the only course of action left open to him. In a last-ditch effort to save himself, Job is willing to play his last card and risk immediate and terrible divine retribution.

In the ancient world (as today) oaths represented the ultimate test of one's honesty. A verbal blessing had the power within itself to effect a concrete experience of blessing. A curse implied in an oath was also understood to have this same power. Once uttered, the oath must be fulfilled. Uttered falsely, the curse for guilt inevitably comes to pass. Thus Job knows that as he utters these oaths, his fate has been decided.

Job is not the only biblical character who, in desperation, "plays a last card." Jacob, facing the ordeal of having to confront his cheated brother, Esau, fights a desperate battle with God before crossing the Jabbok. (See Genesis 32:22-32.) Moses, in a moment of despair over the tasks facing him as the leader in the wilderness, asks God to slay him rather than allow things to continue as they are. (See Numbers 11:10-17.) Abraham arrogantly bargains with God to save Sodom's innocents. (See Genesis 18:22-23.) Jesus himself begs God to spare him the final humiliating "cup" of crucifixion. (See Luke 22:40-43.)

Although none of us has suffered a devastating string of setbacks to match Job's, some of us have experienced suffering that has stymied us. Many of us have found ourselves facing an impasse with no route of escape. At the time, every human resource appeared to fail; and we were left feeling absolutely helpless.

Think back on experiences you have had when you felt your "back was against the wall." Were any of these experiences life threatening? In approaching that moment of total vulnerability, what steps did you take to avert it? Did you, like Job, have a last card to play? If so, what was it? What difference did it make? What sustains us when we know that the next step must be God's, but we do not know what that step will be?

It is not only the old who are wise,
not only the aged who understand what is right (32:9).

11

The Wisdom of Youth
Job 32–34

DIMENSION ONE:
WHAT DOES THE BIBLE SAY?

Answer these questions by reading Job 32

1. Why do Job's friends stop debating with him? (32:1)

2. Why is Elihu angry at Job and his friends? (32:2-3)

3. Why hasn't Elihu spoken before? (32:4)

4. Why does Elihu finally speak up? (32:8-9)

5. What does Elihu plan to do? (32:14)

6. Why can't Elihu wait any longer? (32:18-20)

7. How will Elihu address them? (32:21-22)

Answer these questions by reading Job 33

8. By what power is Elihu inspired? (33:4)

9. What reassurance does Elihu offer Job? (33:6-7)

10. What does Elihu say Job has claimed? (33:9-11)

11. How does Elihu feel about Job's claims? (33:12)

12. Does God speak to mortals? (33:14)

13. What is one way God speaks to mortals? (33:15-16)

14. Why does God send these dreams? (33:17-18)

15. What is another way God speaks to mortals? (33:19)

16. What does the sufferer need in this situation? (33:23)

17. What can the mediator do? (33:24)

18. What is the result of this intercession? (33:26)

19. What does the sufferer then do? (33:27-28)

Answer these questions by reading Job 34

20. What other claims of Job does Elihu cite? (34:5, 6, 9)

21. How does God judge a person? (34:11)

22. Why would it be impossible for God to act unjustly? (34:13-19)

23. How does God treat the mighty? (34:24)

24. Will God render justice in ways that suit Job? (34:33)

25. Why will the wise condemn Job? (34:36-37)

DIMENSION TWO:
WHAT DOES THE BIBLE MEAN?

❏ *Job 32:1-10.* Job's final challenge to God leaves his three friends speechless. No one guilty of sin would dare to risk what Job has. So they realize that nothing they say can possibly sway him. Elihu, a young man from the land of Buz, has apparently heard everything that has happened; and he is furious. He is angry at Job for daring to justify himself rather than God. And Elihu is angry at the friends because they could not silence Job (verses 2-3).

Custom required the young to assume the role of respectful listeners. Elihu makes a point of stressing not only his youth but also his fear of interrupting the older men. Yet Job's outrageous behavior and the others' bumbling responses drive him to speak. Clearly, their age has not guaranteed them the wisdom they need to cope with Job. Nothing but the Spirit of God within a person can provide the insight needed, and the Spirit does not care about age (verses 8-9).

❏ *Job 32:11-14.* Elihu continues to defend what must seem like an unwarranted intrusion. "I gave you your chance," he tells them, "but none of you was up to the task." After analyzing the dispute, Elihu has the advantage of providing the last word on the subject. Their claim to wisdom is bogus; their rebukes fell on deaf ears. Elihu, however, is too clever to make the same mistake. His advice to Job will be quite different and more effective (verse 14).

❏ *Job 32:15-22.* Elihu sees the discomfort of the three friends with satisfaction. He points out how silent they are. They are at a total loss, so why should he wait any longer? Elihu is full of righteous indignation. Like a wineskin ready to burst with the pressure of fermentation, he can no longer contain himself. He must speak. But he promises that, however passionately he may feel, he will speak only the truth.

❑ *Job 33:1-7.* Turning to Job, Elihu attempts to convince him of his sincerity. "Believe me, Job. What I have to say to you is the God-inspired truth. I challenge you to prove me wrong" (verses 3-5). Sarcastically, Elihu assures Job that he has nothing to fear in this new exchange. "After all, I, too, am a mortal. My powers are not, like the terrors of God, paralyzing in their effects" (verse 7).

❑ *Job 33:8-11.* But Elihu himself had heard Job blaspheme. "You say you are pure and sinless and that God is looking for excuses to persecute you. Such accusations cannot be allowed to go unanswered."

❑ *Job 33:12-18.* Elihu launches his attack by repeating Job's shocking assertions. Job's claim to be an innocent victim of God and his assertion that God will not answer him are flatly rebutted by the self-confident young man. Job should realize that God has more than one way of communicating with mortals. Elihu then says God uses nightmares as warnings to wrongdoers. Terrified by the dreams of a guilty conscience, the sinner is finally persuaded to stop sinning and thus save his or her life (verses 15-18).

Dreams are not the only way God communicates. Pain and physical suffering such as Job now knows are also signals from God. The discipline of suffering (claims a man too young to have suffered deeply himself) is the way to return to righteous living. The dying person may yet hope for a reprieve if a mediator or guardian angel will intercede for the sufferer (verse 23). This divine intercession includes paying some kind of ransom. The sufferer can then once again begin to hope and pray for acceptance in the sight of God. And because God is gracious, these prayers are accepted. The redeemed sinner joyfully admitted to receiving far more than is deserved (verses 26-28).

❑ *Job 33:29-33.* "Think of it, Job," he marvels. "Not once but twice, even three times, God will bring the suffering sinner back from the brink of destruction! Don't you see how this applies to you too? If you think that you can rebut this, go ahead and try. Otherwise, keep quiet and let me set you straight."

THE WISDOM OF YOUTH   **91**

❑ *Job 34:1-9.* Elihu returns to the damaging evidence of Job's testimony. Elihu thinks Job's claims are outrageous. Job says he is innocent, robbed by God of his rights and made to seem a liar. "Have you ever in your life seen anyone with the gall to say, as Job says, that it profits one nothing to take delight in God?"

❑ *Job 34:10-20.* Elihu is determined to stamp out this heresy using strange logic. He argues that God cannot possibly be evil or unjust because God, who created the universe and holds all life, also governs what is created. Elihu assumes that no evildoer would ever be in a position to govern (verse 17). History and the Bible itself have proven this assumption false. Elihu claims that God's impartiality is impeccable. The rich and the aristocratic suffer the same fate as any common person (verses 19-20).

❑ *Job 34:21-30.* Job's demands for a hearing are pointless. God sees everything that goes on, and no evidence is new to God. "How arrogant to expect God to set up an appointment to hear your puny claims" (verse 23). God's justice is given without any unnecessary or bureaucratic delays. Sinners will be struck down without warning (verses 24-25). Strangely, Elihu implies that sometimes this system of justice breaks down. Sometimes God ignores injustice. But who can dare to condemn God for taking an action that is hard to understand (verse 29)?

❑ *Job 34:31-37.* Elihu mocks Job's right to hold God to any pattern of action. "Do you expect to be acquitted solely on your own terms?" Job has a choice. He can confess and receive forgiveness, or he can continue his fruitless rebellion. Which will it be (verse 33)?

Elihu is not optimistic about his efforts to convert Job. He claims that anyone with an ounce of sense will despise Job for being a fool. And facing this failure, the young man turns vicious. Elihu feels Job should be tested to the end. That is, Job should suffer all that there is to suffer. For the unrepentant sinner is the ultimate threat to the dignity and credibility of the God-fearing.

DIMENSION THREE:
WHAT DOES THE BIBLE MEAN TO ME?

Job 32:9—It Is Not Only the Old Who Are Wise

In introducing the character of Elihu, much is made over the fact of his youth. In ancient societies such as Israel, wisdom and authority were usually vested in a group of powerful persons identified as elders. Age brings with it experience and a balanced perspective on the ups and downs of life that the causes and enthusiasm of youth never seem to achieve. Scripture, and the wisdom tradition in particular, testifies to the importance of youthful respect for what previous generations have learned. For example, the Book of Proverbs is full of good advice originally addressed to young men by their wisdom teachers and elders. (See Proverbs 4.)

On the other hand, the Bible also witnesses to a tradition that questions the validity of wisdom and authority established by humans. This tradition asserts that the Spirit of God working within persons bestows wisdom and ability. When Elihu makes this claim in Job 32:8-9, he bases his right to speak on a tradition that allows for and honors the appearance of wisdom where it is least expected.

This same awareness of the Spirit's impartiality allows the psalmist to claim that "I have more insight than all my teachers. . . . I have more understanding than the elders, / for I obey your precepts" (Psalm 119:99-100). Similarly, Paul was acutely aware that his understanding of the gospel and his ability to preach it had nothing to do with his age, his learning, or his abilities. Speaking to the church at Corinth, he rejects "eloquence or superior wisdom" as a legitimate means of conversion. Instead, he relies entirely on the "demonstration of the Spirit's power." (See 1 Corinthians 2:1-5.)

When has your own experience borne out the claim that "it is not only the old who are wise"? When young people show unusual wisdom and insight, how do you account for it? Do you think of these expressions of wisdom as evidence of divine inspiration? Why or why not? How do you account for lapses of wisdom on the part of young and old alike?

THE WISDOM OF YOUTH
93

Finally, how valid is the claim of the self-confident young man Elihu? How much wisdom and inspiration do you feel lie behind his words to Job and the three friends? Do you think the author of the Elihu speeches takes this claim seriously? Is the character of Elihu meant to be a parody of the wise youth?

Job 33:14—God Speaks in One Way, and in Two

God has tormented Job with such awful nightmares that Job would rather die than keep suffering this mental torture. (See Job 7:14-15.) Elihu's point is that these dreams are the way God has chosen to communicate with Job. Their purpose is to scare him so that he will be driven to repent and be restored to life. (See Job 33:15-18.)

The significance of dreams as vehicles for divine revelation is a prominent biblical motif. The young Samuel warns Eli as a result of a revelation received in a night vision. (See 1 Samuel 3:2-14.) Joseph, the youngest and much beloved son of Jacob, reported a prophetic dream to his older brothers. His brothers then set in motion a series of events that ultimately fulfilled that very dream. (See Genesis 37:5-11.) Both Joseph and the young Daniel are considered wise because of their ability to interpret the dreams of others—dreams meant to serve as warnings. (See Genesis 40–41; Daniel 4.)

Has your experience borne out the claims of Elihu that dreams, especially bad dreams, are a means of divine communication? Psychologists tell us that our dreams reveal much about us and our feelings. They reveal (in hidden or symbolic fashion) knowledge that is normally not accessible to us. Would you agree? Do all your dreams seem instructive? Or are some dreams more powerful in their effect than others? When has a dream moved you to repentance?

But those who suffer he delivers in their suffering;
he speaks to them in their affliction (36:15).

12

The Lessons of Affliction
Job 35–37

DIMENSION ONE:
WHAT DOES THE BIBLE SAY?

Answer these questions by reading Job 35

1. Which question of Job's does Elihu quote? (35:3)

2. Where should Job look for an answer? (35:5)

3. Do Job's actions either injure or benefit God? (35:6-8)

4. What do the multitudes who cry out against oppression fail to do? (35:10-12)

5. Why doesn't God respond to Job's complaints? (35:16)

6. On whose behalf does Elihu speak? (36:2)

7. How does Elihu describe himself? (36:4)

8. How does God treat the wicked? (36:6)

9. How does God treat the righteous? (36:7)

10. What does God do when the righteous are afflicted? (36:9-10)

11. How do the godless respond to affliction? (36:13)

12. What happens to those who do not learn the lessons of affliction? (36:14)

13. How has God treated Job in the past? (36:16)

14. What does Elihu claim Job has chosen? (36:21)

15. What does Elihu advise Job to do? (36:24)

16. What is the work of God described by Elihu? (36:27-30)

Answer these questions by reading Job 37

17. To what does Elihu compare the thunder? (37:4-5)

18. What wonderful thing does God do? (37:6-10)

19. Why does God command the elements? (37:13)

20. Which of God's wondrous works should be the subjects of Job's meditation? (37:15-18)

21. Where does God come from? (37:22)

22. What are the characteristics of the God humans seek? (37:23)

23. How does God treat those who think they are wise? (37:24)

DIMENSION TWO:
WHAT DOES THE BIBLE MEAN?

❏ *Job 35:1-8.* Elihu, who has been silent for so long, now has plenty of advice. "Job cries for justice, does he? Well, how just are you, Job, when you insist that you are in the right and God is unjust? How just are you when you question whether there is anything to be gained by being faithful?" (verses 2-3). Elihu is the real theologian of the group. Obviously, he has spent many hours speculating on the nature and purposes of God. He tells Job to look above himself and to consider how far beyond him the reality of God is. "Can you possibly think that your petty little actions make any difference to God?" he asks. He tells Job that God cares nothing for our feeble gestures of worship or defiance.

❏ *Job 35:9-15.* "Sinners like you cause trouble, Job. Oppression is multiplied, and the victims of oppression cry out against it; yet their cries are in vain." Elihu reasons that being self-centered and proud accounts for God's silence in the face of oppression. To cry out against oppression is simply not enough. One must cry out for God and rely totally on God's mercy. In other words, the impulse to seek immediate relief must be checked and the lessons of affliction thoroughly learned (verses 10-11).

Because of sinners like Job, the undisciplined howls of all the suffering people will not reach God's ears, just as Job's empty outbursts are not heard. After all, who is Job to complain about being forsaken in court? Who is Job to assault God's justice simply because he sees transgressions go unpunished (verses 14-15)?

❏ *Job 36:1-4.* The more he talks, the more confident Elihu becomes. "Be patient, and listen—for I speak on God's behalf." Elihu claims that his research has been exhaustive, so what he shares with them is absolutely reliable. As one who is perfect (complete) in knowledge, Elihu can be counted on not to leave anything out (verse 4).

❏ *Job 36:5-12.* Elihu now launches into his basic thesis: Affliction is a divine discipline. Elihu's God, mighty in understanding as well as in strength, can be trusted to deal equitably with everyone. God will certainly dispense with the wicked, but the righteous are the apple of God's eye. Should righteous persons fall into error, the Lord will make them aware of their sins and teach them and purify them through their suffering.

Ghastly as it is, affliction can help open the ears of sinners (verse 10). Those who were formerly deaf to the divine demands are suddenly made to hear them. At long last these persons learn to see themselves as they really are. With this new knowledge, the sufferer is offered the choice to repent and live or cling to ignorance and meet a violent end (verses 11-12).

❑ *Job 36:13-16.* Unfortunately, not everyone responds to this treatment in the appropriate way. The unrepentant will nurture their anger against God and refuse to acknowledge their dependence on God's help. These sinners die young (verses 13-14). What could have become a means of salvation thereby becomes a means of destruction. Elihu reminds Job that once before he had been delivered from affliction and restored to a life of pleasurable abundance (verse 16).

❑ *Job 36:17-23.* Elihu accuses Job of being full of the fruits of his own wickedness. God's justice has him by the throat. He must deal with and overcome the temptation to nurse his anger and close his mind. If he does not, he will die. Like other sufferers, Job has a crucial choice to make. How will he deal with suffering? Will he accept the lessons of affliction and learn from them (verse 21)? And what if he does not? God, the Master Teacher, does not need a person to be his teacher. A person cannot tell God what to do (verses 22-23).

❑ *Job 36:24-33.* Still hoping to sway Job from his uncompromising position, Elihu bursts into a hymn of praise for God the ruler of the universe. "Don't dwell on your misery, Job. Instead, think of the Creator and God's mighty works. Look around you at the world of nature and marvel at God's amazing wisdom and power. Who else could draw up water from the earth into the air and then return it in the form of rain? Can anyone understand the awesome circling of the clouds, the ominous roar of thunder, or the destructive power of lightning (verses 27-30)? Mind you, these marvels are not simply for entertainment. They are a means of divine judgment and grace."

❏ *Job 37:1-13.* Elihu quivers at the thought of such marvels. He tells Job to listen to the thunder of God's voice. Job must heed the wonder of winter when snow and ice cover the earth. When foul weather forces both humans and beasts indoors, they are helpless to act. They observe what God does without effort (verses 6-10). Unlike unruly mortals, the forces of nature obey their Creator who manipulates them for the sake of disciplining sinners, rewarding the righteous, or blessing the land (verses 12-13).

❏ *Job 37:14-20.* Elihu vindictively challenges Job's understanding of how the universe works. "Do you claim to understand all this? Could you duplicate God's work in any way? If you can, tell us. Unlike yourself, we are at a total loss to know what to say." Elihu assures Job that he himself would never dare to take on God as Job has claimed he is willing to do. Such an accusation would be an invitation to disaster (verses 19-20).

❏ *Job 37:21-24.* When God's terrifying storm of judgment has passed and the sky clears, a blinding light appears. Out of the north comes a fabulous glow of gold. God, more magnificent than all our dreams, remains forever out of reach for humans. God does not regard with favor persons who think of themselves as wise.

Elihu's speeches have now prepared both Job and the reader for the appearance of God in the next chapter.

DIMENSION THREE:
WHAT DOES THE BIBLE MEAN TO ME?

Job 36:15—God Delivers the Afflicted

In the previous lesson we saw that Elihu considered suffering, particularly physical pain, as one way God attempts to communicate with mortals. (See Job 33:19-22.) Now we see Elihu returning to the theme of divine discipline as he continues his dispute with Job. Beginning with Job 36:5 and following, Elihu develops this theme in more detail.

God, strong and wise, punishes the wicked with death and exalts the righteous so that they live like kings (verse 7). If the righteous should stumble, as Job certainly must have, then

God allows them to suffer the consequences of their evil deeds. In this way God uses pain as an effective form of instruction. Those who respond humbly to the harsh lessons of affliction are restored to health and prosperity. Those who continue to be angry and rebel against God's counsel will quickly perish, having never understood the true cause of their ordeal (verse 12).

In short, God's motive in allowing anyone to suffer is actually love. God's hope is that the sinner may yet be persuaded to repent and return to a life of obedience.

Paul makes a similar argument when he speaks of God giving sinners up to their sins as a last resort. Presumably, if they experience the full impact of their own wickedness, they may learn what they have refused to learn, even though the truth about God was evident for all to see and understand. (See Romans 1:18-32.)

Another famous biblical example of divine discipline is the story of Jonah, a Hebrew called by God to minister to a hated enemy people. Jonah's refusal to respond to the call results in suffering and danger, not only for himself but also for others. Finally, just when he expects to find release from the obligations of obedience in death, a new trial awaits him. Jonah's ride toward dry land in the belly of a great fish is the kind of affliction by which the afflicted are delivered. Recognizing this, Jonah sings a psalm of thanksgiving while still inside the fish. When he is actually deposited on shore, Jonah is finally ready to profit from the hard lessons he has learned (Jonah 1–2).

Today, we speak of "blessings in disguise" as a way of describing difficult or painful experiences that eventually are recognized as being instructive or a means of grace. Reflect on your own experiences. How often and how well have you been "instructed" by affliction? Would you agree with Elihu that God permits suffering out of a motive of love and concern? When has a painful experience led you to repentance or conversion? How often do you "cherish anger" against God as a response to suffering? Elihu, like the three friends, assumes that Job is suffering because of sin. We, the readers, know that Job has not sinned; yet God permits Job to suffer. Review the conditions under which God agrees to this kind of treatment for Job. (See Job 1:6-12.) Would you classify this kind of test as "divine discipline"? Why, or why not?

Job 35:10—Where Is God My Maker?

An important point in the Elihu speeches is that prayer is an appropriate response to suffering. To prepare for discussion of this issue, carefully reread the following passages: Job 33:19-28; 34:31-32; 35:9-13; 36:24–37:13. For each passage, try to answer these questions: What is the situation of the sufferer? Pain? Sin? Oppression? Does Elihu suggest a cause for that situation arising? Is a particular type of prayer recommended? Is the actual content of the prayer suggested? What does Elihu say will be the outcome of this type of prayer?

Now compare what Elihu says about prayer as a response to affliction with what you have learned from your own experience. Do you find it more or less difficult to pray in situations of suffering? Does suffering spur you to more fervent prayer or does it make you angry, depressed, or cynical? Are certain types of prayer impossible for you at such times? If so, which types? Would you say that Job "prayed" in response to his affliction? Would Elihu say that Job had "prayed"? Would you agree that Job's method of approaching God was appropriate for his situation?

My ears had heard of you
but now my eyes have seen you (42:5).

—— 13 ——
When God Asks
the Questions
Job 38–42

DIMENSION ONE:
WHAT DOES THE BIBLE SAY?

Answer these questions by reading Job 38:1-38

1. How does the Lord appear to Job? (38:1)

2. How does the Lord describe Job's words? (38:2)

3. What is the Lord's challenge to Job? (38:3)

4. For what nine parts of creation does God claim responsibility?

_____ (38:4)

_____ (38:8)

_____ (38:12)

_____ (38:17)

_____ (38:19)

_____ (38:22)

_____ (38:25)

_____ (38:31-32)

_____ (38:34-35)

Answer this question by reading Job 38:39–Job 39:30

5. For what eleven creatures is God responsible?

_____ (38:39)

_____ (38:41)

_____ (39:1)

_____ (39:1)

_____ (39:1)

_____ (39:5)

_____ (39:9)

_____ (39:13)

_____ (39:19)

_____ (39:26)

_____ (39:27)

Answer these questions by reading Job 40–41

6. What is Job's answer to the Lord? (40:4-5)

7. What is the Lord's accusation against Job? (40:8)

8. When will God acknowledge that Job can vindicate himself? (40:10-14)

9. What two powerful monsters has God made? (40:15; 41:1)

Answer these questions by reading Job 42

10. What four things does Job acknowledge in his response to God? (42:2, 3, 5, 6)

11. What does the Lord say to Eliphaz? (42:7)

12. What must Eliphaz, Bildad, and Zophar do to avoid divine judgment? (42:8)

13. Who has spoken correctly about the Lord? (42:8)

14. When are Job's fortunes restored? (42:10)

15. How much of Job's fortune is restored to him? (42:10)

16. What blessings does Job receive? (42:11-13)

17. Why are Job's three daughters unique? (42:15)

18. How many generations of descendants does Job finally live to see? (42:16)

DIMENSION TWO:
WHAT DOES THE BIBLE MEAN?

❏ *Job 38:1-3.* Elihu's words are followed abruptly by the appearance of Israel's God, Yahweh (LORD in the New International Version). God appears in a tempest or whirlwind. Sternly, God demands to know who is speaking so ignorantly of the divine design for governing the universe. Job is to prepare himself for a monumental battle of wits. For it is God who will ask the questions and not Job.

❏ *Job 38:4-38.* Here the Lord begins a long series of sarcastic rhetorical questions. God knows Job cannot possibly answer them. Formulated to "put Job in his place," these questions force Job to deal directly with God. This confrontation dramatically alters all his previous ideas about the nature of God and the divine purposes for the work of creation.

God begins by asking where Job was when the earth's foundations were laid. Job has spoken as if he himself were there to witness the event. After all, hasn't he claimed to know what justice is and how the world should be governed (verses 4-7)? Does Job know who keeps the heaving seas, like a baby in swaddling clothes? Who contained the sea so that the dark waters of chaos could never overwhelm God's orderly creation (verses 8-11)?

Or perhaps Job has the power to command the sun to rise daily and shed its light abroad so that evildoers are exposed (verses 12-15). And what about the deepest recesses of the sea where the secrets of life and death lay hidden? Has Job descended to those fearsome depths and walked through the gates that lead to the nether world? If he has, God would like to hear about it (verses 16-18).

Next, God asks Job if he knows the abodes of light and darkness. Separated in the act of Creation (Genesis 1:3-5), light and darkness were given appointed times to appear—day and night. They were also given appointed places to await those appointed times. Job, who thinks he possesses the wisdom of Adam, should know these secret times and places (verses 19-21).

And what about those marvelous instruments of divine judgment, snow and hail? Does Job know where God keeps this remarkable stuff stored? Can Job find his way to God's arsenal where lightning bolts are kept? Here also the fierce east wind stays hidden, waiting to be unleashed upon earth's sinful inhabitants (verses 22-24). Does Job realize that storms are not random violence? They are carefully planned and executed. They even provide moisture for uninhabited regions so that the lowest forms of plant life may thrive (verses 25-27). Even if Job knew where to find the elements of weather, could he ever hope to create them? Who, asks the Lord, actually brings these wonders to birth? "Do you, Job?"

Can Job guide the constellations in their journeys across the heavens? Does he understand how these heavenly bodies operate (verses 21-33)? God challenges Job to command the clouds to burst at his will and rain down torrents of water on the earth. Will bolts of lightning snap to attention when he calls?

❏ *Job 38:39–39:30.* From the mysteries of Creation, God proceeds to question Job on the mysteries of the animal kingdom. Who, the Almighty asks, ensures that the voracious appetites of the young lions who roam the wilderness are satisfied? Who makes sure that the raven will find enough food for her hungry young? Does Job? Does Job stand loving watch at the birth of the young mountain goat? Can he watch over the wild donkey who forages in the wilderness? Can he tame the wild and free-spirited ox? Can he guarantee the survival of the witless ostrich who leaves her unhatched young where they can be trodden on or devoured by wild beasts? What about the strength of the warhorse who rushes joyfully into battle? Can Job take credit for that? Can he explain why the eagle, who makes her home in the treacherous cliffs, can soar vast distances above the ground and still spot prey far below?

❏ *Job 40:1–8.* What does Job really know? What can Job really do? Can a hasty and ill-advised critic like Job argue successfully with his Creator? If Job still thinks he is ready for this confrontation, let him respond to these questions! Of course, Job knows that the battle has been lost with the first shot fired. Stunned by this vision of overwhelming power and intelligence, Job can merely stammer. "I am nobody! What can I possibly say to you?" But once again God issues the command to engage in verbal combat. "Prepare yourself, Job. I have more questions for the man who wishes to justify himself at my expense!"

❏ *Job 40:9–14.* God now specifies the conditions under which Job may be vindicated. "Do as I do!" demands the Almighty. "Clothe yourself in splendor. Execute judgment on the proud. Trample the wicked into the dust. Send them all packing to the place of oblivion. Then I will allow you to challenge my administration of the universe!"

❏ *Job 40:15–41:34.* Finally, God presents Job with the most bizarre and frightening of all his works: the behemoth and the leviathan. The behemoth is a grass-eating mammal of immense strength. Fearless and unconquerable, this beast has bones of bronze and limbs of iron. But it is still, like Job, a creature and therefore subject to divine direction. The leviathan, the menacing sea serpent, tempts mortals to engage in a battle they are doomed to lose. The leviathan is the epitome of evil and terror.

❏ *Job 42:1-6.* This is enough! Job has seen more than he can possibly digest. God, his maker and teacher, has set before him the entire "curriculum" of creation in a demonstration of power and wisdom. Job fully realizes the reality of a truth he had been taught to affirm. Nothing can thwart God's purposes! Repeating God's question to him (verse 3), Job attempts an answer. He acknowledges that he is the "guilty" party. He, Job, had dared to speak of things he knew nothing about.

God's command that Job be the one to answer has brought the rebel to a moment of truth. God is infinitely more than Job had ever imagined, while Job is infinitely less. Everything he had previously heard or been taught now seems insignificant in the face of an actual encounter with the Almighty. Seeing God has meant seeing himself as he really is. Frail and ignorant, Job no longer finds anything in himself worth vindicating. He is finally content with a response of simple repentance.

❏ *Job 42:7-17.* In an instant we find ourselves transported to the world of the prologue. These verses are an epilogue, also in prose. Job's confession is followed by God's rebuke to Eliphaz and his cohorts. (Notice that there is no mention of Elihu.) Ironically, the friends' spirited defense of the Almighty has gone unappreciated, just as Job had predicted it would. (See Job 13:7-12.) But Job's attacks on God are said to be correct. Eliphaz and his cohorts' only hope is to make speedy restitution with a sacrifice. They must also implore the prayers of Job on their behalf, for this righteousness (as before) makes him a good intercessor.

Job, on the other hand, must cast aside his feelings of having been mistreated. He must offer prayers for three men who in the name of friendship had become loathsome enemies. Once this act of divine justice is carried out, Job once again receives abundant blessings.

WHEN GOD ASKS THE QUESTIONS   **109**

DIMENSION THREE:
WHAT DOES THE BIBLE MEAN TO ME?

Job 38:1-3—God's Answer to Job

In the end, God does respond to Job's challenge. But in responding, God makes it clear that God will set the terms of the encounter! Job's questions and loud complaints are never dealt with at all. Nor is Job ever informed of the Accuser's wager as the ultimate cause of his misfortunes. Instead, God responds to Job's challenge by posing another, entirely different, set of questions. These questions give Job a vivid glimpse into the mystery and grandeur of God's creative activity.

Stunned into silence, Job realizes that he never really understood the issue. His concern for personal vindication was argued from the faulty premise that suffering must be the result of sin. In contrast to what he has just witnessed, Job's furious efforts to seek justice on his own behalf seem petty and irrelevant. For along with the revelation he has received of God's majesty and wisdom comes a further revelation. Job's questions are not God's questions.

Job learns that an encounter with God is answer enough. And God's willingness to encounter Job in his struggle to recover his good name is vindication enough. When Job finally repents, it is not because he believes himself to be a sinner. It is because he has discovered his own lack of wisdom and power.

Job's dramatic encounter with God is not something we often see in the lives of faithful Christians today. Yet all of us must struggle with the question of what it means to be dependent creatures who lack the power to vindicate ourselves. Job refused to accept stock answers from his friends. But he could not recognize that something other than simple justice might be at stake.

Most of us do not have either Job's personal integrity or his level of feeling and expression. We are pale by comparison. But we must remember in our anger, confusion, and pain that we—like Job—do not have all the facts. Our responses to pain and loss, honest though they may be, are shaped by faulty knowledge and a limited understanding of God.

Job's Answer to Us: Job and the Study of Scripture

Job found God, but that encounter was very different from the way Job thought it would be. Job discovered that in the communication between Creator and creature, it is God who asks the questions!

When you began your study of Job, you were asked to reflect on your previous experiences with the book and character of Job. How did these experiences shape your questions and expectations for the experience of studying Job in depth—perhaps for the first time? Can you remember now what those initial expectations were? What were the questions you hoped to find answers for in the Book of Job? Were any of these questions answered? Or did you—like Job—find a string of unanswerable questions? Were your own opinions about the nature of God or Scripture challenged by the reality of studying this most remarkable of books?

We know that Job has endured in the memories of Jews and Christians as a model of both integrity and patience. Perhaps it is time we recognize that in this man we find a model for the student of the Bible. The serious Bible student maintains a sense of honesty and personal integrity in the dialogue with Scripture. But he or she also recognizes that disciplined study requires an attitude of repentance as well. Job's answer to us is actually an invitation. It is an invitation to "gird up the loins" of our hearts and minds and prepare to answer the questions that Scripture puts to us!

VISUALIZING THE STRUCTURE OF JOB

Prologue
(1–2)

Job's Lament
(3)

First Round of Dialogues
(4–14)

Second Round of Dialogues
(15–21)

Third Round of Dialogues
(22–27)

Wisdom Hymn
(28)

Job's Final Appeal
(29–31)

Elihu Speeches
(32–37)

God's Response
(38:1–42:6)

Epilogue
(42:7-17)

poetry

probably later insertion